I0437909

WHAT WE BLACKS NEED TO DO

THE FIRST BOOK IN A THREE BOOK SERIES

by
James J. Hankins

AuthorHouse™
1663 Liberty Drive, Suite 200
Bloomington, IN 47403
www.authorhouse.com
Phone: 1-800-839-8640

© 2007 James J. Hankins. All rights reserved.

No part of this book may be reproduced, stored in
a retrieval system, or transmitted by any means
without the written permission of the author.

First published by AuthorHouse 11/5/2007

ISBN: 978-1-4343-4697-1 (sc)

Library of Congress Control Number: 2007908206

Printed in the United States of America
Bloomington, Indiana

This book is printed on acid-free paper.

DEDICATED TO

1. My Three Families:

    The Bellamys - Matriarch, Mrs. Mary Holden Bellamy.

    The Hankins - Patriarch, Mr. Charles Henry Hankins

    The McLeans - Matriarch, Mrs. Faldenia McLean Hankins

2. My immediate Family.

    *Father, Edward Hankins, Barber& Entrepreneur

    Mother, Faldenia McLean Hankins, Special Education Teacher

    *Sister, Barbara Hankins Simmons, Middle School Teacher

    Brother, Charles Hankins, Auto Mechanic & Electrician

    *Sister, Alice Hankins Jackson Elementary School Teacher

    *Sister, Caroline Hankins Oliphant, Vocational Rehabilitation Counselor& Drivers License Examiner

*Deceased.

Special Cousin, Reginald Armstrong, Computer
   Sales Manager
Wife, Faye Bellamy Hankins, College Professor &
   Certified Public Accountant
Son, James Edward Oliver Hankins II, Honor
   Student, President of the Student Government
   & Athlete -12th Grade

3. Mrs. Eunice Boykin, a good friend, neighbor and
distinguished retired English Teacher. Mrs. Boykin's
explanations made revisiting the rules of grammar
easy. Mr. & Mrs. Boykin's children, Hartford and
Pamela, were in the first group of Black students to
enroll in all White schools in Wilmington, NC.

This book is written for all ages. It contains no profanity (cussing). It is rated G.

The late Dr. Martin Luther King Jr. had a very large vocabulary (used a lot of words). His speeches and writings gave us a positive message and also taught us some new words to add to our vocabulary. Dr. King used what we call "big words" and "everyday words"after them to explain their meaning. When you listen to his sermons, you will hear his Father, "Daddy King," in the background saying, "Make it plain." As a teacher, I will follow the example set by a greater teacher, Dr. King. I will share with you my opinion of some positive solutions to our many problems and, hopefully, add some new words to your vocabulary.

I plan to donate 30% of the profits from this "Best Seller" to charities and organizations that support Black people and our struggles to achieve equality.

**THIS BOOK IS BEING WRITTEN IN THREE VOLUMES.
EACH VOLUME WILL CONTAIN THREE CHAPTERS.**

Foreword

I STILL REMEMBER THE time when my father said he was planning to write a book. "To me, my father was not a person to write a book. He tended to carry the policy made famous by President Theodore Roosevelt, "speak softly, and carry a big stick." He has always been one to unabashedly speak his mind, but rarely has he ever been lengthy about his opinions. So this emergence in him of a need to write a book was not only a surprise but was also a breath of fresh air. Working in the school system, my father had many complaints that he voiced and even wrote about, but this book: is his chance to get it all out. There have been many heated discussions over material that he has put in the book but this is his endeavor; so, what he says is precisely what he thinks. I ask you as you read this book to keep in mind the background of my father. He's a man who joined the army to go to college, who graduated from North Carolina A&T State University, who fought for civil rights, and who taught for nearly 3 decades. With such a background it should not be surprising that he has very strong and controversial opinions about nearly everything. Some of my own opinions, as well as my mother's, directly conflict with things that will be said in this book, but we still stand behind his decision and support him 100%. So as you are reading, you will find stuff that will make you laugh (some of it at my own expense), stuff that will make you think, and even stuff that will make you mad, but what I am absolutely sure you will find is the story and opinions of a man who has been through it all and is deeply passionate about his beliefs. Enjoy this read, I guarantee it's a good one.

James E.O. Hankins II

Hats I have worn and some I am presently wearing.

♦ St. Thomas Catholic Primary School
♦ Alter Server - St. Thomas Catholic Church
♦ Usher - St. Thomas and St. Mary Catholic Church
♦ Boy Scout
♦ Vise- President, New Hanover County Youth NAACP
♦ Paper carrier for The Wilmington Journal
♦ Varsity Football Player
♦ Williston Senior High- Class of 1964
♦ Roman Catholic
♦ U S Army - Sgt. E-5
♦ Active voter - 95%
♦ North Carolina A & T State University - Class of 1971
♦ Real Estate Broker

- Carpenter- Lead and Construction Foreman
- House Painter
- Residential Lister for an Appraisal Company
- Teacher
- Middle School Coach - Football, Basketball and Baseball
- Union Member-American Federation of Teachers
- Master Gardener
- Christmas and Pecan Tree Farmer
- Community Leader
- Membership-Chairman, New Hanover County Branch NAACP -
- Husband
- Finance Committee St. Mary Catholic Church
- Father
- Uncle
- Realtor
- Volunteer voter register
- Precinct official - Democrat Party
- Volunteer tutor - New Hanover County NAACP
- President- New Hanover County Branch NAACP
- Life Member - NAACP

- Friends of The Wilmington Journal Committee
- Entrepreneur - J. Hankins Realty
- License General Contractor
- Writer
- North Carolina A&T State University Alumni Association
- Estate Administrator
- Power of Attorney for a Family friend
- Care Giver
- Court Appointed Guardian
- Construction Manager- Youth Build

James J. Hankins is a retired vocational teacher. He had to sit in the back of the bus and suffered other types of discrimination of his generation. He graduated from an all Black high school in 1964 ,then predominantly Black N.C. A&T State University in 1971. He was a member and leader in his local branch of the NAACP for over fifty years. This is the first volume of his three volume book discussing proven solutions to the many problems facing the Black race.

CONTENTS

CHAPTER 1
WHAT OUR BLACK FAMILIES NEED TO DO.

"CHILDREN, OBEY YOUR PARENTS in the Lord, for that is right. Honor thy father and mother - such is the first commandment with a promise - that it mayest be long-lived upon the earth. And you fathers, do not provoke your children to anger, but rear them in the discipline and admonition of the Lord."

THE PROBLEMS:

THE GENERAL PROBLEMS:
In some two, parent families, we find problems because the husband and wife have not:

1. Reached an agreement on how to live with each other.

2. Pooled their two pay checks into one bank account.

3. Made a budget for paying bills.

4. Made a list of who will do which jobs inside the house and the yard.

5. Decided who will gas up and be in charge of maintaining the cars.

6. Decided who will make out the menu, shop for groceries and cook.

7. Decided who will wash dishes and what nights.

8. Decided who will handle the checkbook, savings account and investments.

9. Decided if it is better to rent or buy a house.

10. Decided who will pick out the new appliances and furniture.

11. Decided if they are going to church and which church.

12. Decided to have children or how to rear them.

13. Decided who will check homework, sign report cards, meet the teachers and attend PTA.

14. Decided who will give that talk about drugs and sex.

15. Decided who will plan vacations and choose the place.

16. Decided who will take and pick up the children for ball practice and other activities.

17. Decided who will talk to their children's friends before that first date.

18. Decided who will help their children choose their college and career.

19. Decided if they will vote and be active in community affairs.

20. Decided if they will continue to upgrade their education.

In the single parent family, these problems can become larger because the older children must help with these decisions.

We find some of the following problems with some of our Black Elementary, Middle and High School students:

1. They do not take their book to and from school.

2. They do not do homework.

3. They do not take notes in class.

4. They do not take part in classroom discussions.

5. They do not allow themselves any time to think. For example - A student gets up at 7:00 am - turns on the TV and watches it while he is making his bed and putting his room in order- goes to the bathroom-raps, sings or listens to the radio while washing up and grooming - back to his room to dress in front of the TV - eats his breakfast with the radio or TV - puts on his radio headset and walks to the bus stop - talks to his friends at the bus stop and on the ride to school -talks to his friends and listens to teachers during school - exits school bus while putting on radio headset - cuts on TV, plays video games, plays basketball or surfs the Internet until dinner - talks to family during dinner or takes a folding table and his plate to watch TV - does homework - prepare for bed - then falls asleep in bed with the TV still on.

6. They do not watch educational programs on TV.

7. They do not read newspapers, except the sports, clothes, sales and TV section.

8. They have not decided on his or her career goal.

9. They use broken English and profanity as a defiance to authority.

10. They place too much importance on their clothes, hairstyles and accessories.

11. They spend too much time talking and listening to people who don't have their best interest in mind.

12. They do not go to church: so, they don't know the importance of Faith, Hope and Love.

13. And some feel that studying and making good grades is "Acting White."

THE COMMUNICATIONS PROBLEMS:
Far too many families expect other family members to read their minds. You tell a family member to do something, and he does it. You say it was not done right, and he asks, "What else do you want me to do?" You say, "can't you see?" With those three words you are making a statement that is questioning his intelligence, competence and dedication. You also failed to answer his legitimate (reasonable) question.

An argument is sure to follow as the family member defends his lack of ability to do everything the way you want it, without any directions from you.

THE PROBLEM WITH LEAVING THE EDUCATIONAL RESPONSIBILITIES UP TO THE STUDENTS AND THE SCHOOL SYSTEM:

Many of our parents leave all the educational decisions up to their children and the school system. In the old system that we had before the 70s, you could count on the home room teacher, the guidance counselors and the English teachers to explain credits and how many were required to graduate. Today, students will see their home base teacher about four to six times a year for about 20 minutes each time. If you want to see a counselor, you have to make an appointment. Some counselors spend more time discussing drug and family problems than on study habits and courses needed to enter certain occupations. Most counselors, although they lack the credentials, act as if they are psychologists. The English teachers don't have time to talk about credits because they must spend most of their time preparing their students for the end of grade test or suffer the blame if too many of their students fail. Most school systems will print beautiful brochures telling you that every child has a counselor and advisor to advise him or her but that is mostly a public relations scheme.

THE PROBLEM OF PARENTS NOT
MEETING OR BEING AWARE OF THE
PEOPLE DEVELOPING THE CURRICULUM,
REDISTRICTING, TEACHING, GUIDING AND
DISCIPLINING THEIR CHILDREN:

A large number of parents can name seven or more players on the L.A. Lakers, Atlanta Braves, N.Y. Jets and characters on "All My Children", General Hospital" and "As The World Turns." If you ask these same parents to name just five of the men and women teaching their child this school year, you may not receive an answer. What is more important, how many points Allen Iverson is averaging per game or your son's or daughter's grade point average in the four or more classes he or she is taking?

PARENT TEST (Please answer these questions on your children's school system)

1. Name the Chairman of the Board of Education

_____

2. Name the Superintendent

_____

3. Name the Principal

_____

4. Give the number of his or her school bus_____,
School phone number_____

5. What is the school bus driver's name

_____

& number to call if the bus is late after school?

_____

6. If elementary school, name the teacher

_____

Teacher Assistant

_____

Counselor

_____

PE Teacher

_____

Art Teacher

_____

7. If Middle school, fill in time, teacher, lunch and subject:

Period	Teacher	Subject

Counselor

_____

8. If High school - same as middle school

Period	Teacher	Subject

Counselor

_____

9. To graduate from high school, your child, must complete how many credits in each subject?

English	
Math	
Science	
Social Studies	
Health & PE	
Second Language	
Art	
Music	
Computer Skills	
Electives	

10. What is the SAT?

_____

11. What is the minimum score required by your State Public University Systems?

_____

12. What are the admissions requirements for your Community College system?

_____

_____

_____

13. What is the Advanced Placement Program and how can your child become a part of it?

_____

14. How many credits does your high school child have now (_____) and how many should he or she have (_____)?

15. What are your child's plans after high school?

_____

_____

_____

How much money have you saved toward those plans? $_____

16. Can you borrow money to send your child to college?_____. If yes, where do you find this information?_____

17. What is your child's ranking in his or her class overall?

_____

18. What is your child's best subject?

_____

Worst?

_____

19. What is the estimated cost to send your child to your State University for one year?_____

Community College?_____

20. What percentage of students from your child's High School have been accepted into your State University System?_____

THE LANGUAGE PROBLEM:

The profanity (cussing) coming from adults and children is a serious problem. It is not a sign of being macho, hip or cool. It is saying I do not respect myself or any one in hearing range. These words are being picked up by children as young as 16 months and repeated. If children hear it on TV or radio and then from you, their hero, they know it is ok to repeat. Cussing at one time was a man's way of showing how "tough" he was, but today, 2003, some ladies cuss as much or more than the men. One in every fourth word uttered by some pre-teens and teens is a cuss word. The billion dollar entertainment industries that produce and sell to ages 12 to 25 use as much cussing as they can to keep the attention of these paying customers. Some four and seven letter words are repeated over and over so much that I wonder if the so- called writer of that filthy script has ever opened a Thesaurus (a book that group like words together). As Blacks living in a racist society and competing with Whites for jobs and opportunities, one cuss word from us could give the white employer, what some really want, a legitimate opportunity to remove our names from the list.

THE DRESS PROBLEM:
Parents and children have almost always had different taste in clothes, but today that is not the case for some. Certain under garments that were made to wear under your clothes are now being shown to the public. As a Teacher, I had to tell students, boys and girls, to pull up their pants and button their blouse or shirt. I could see where some of them got their fashion tips when we had open house for parents. I had the authority to correct my students, but no one had authority to correct the parents. We spend too much money on clothes and place too much importance on them.

THE DRUG PROBLEM:
In September, 2001, The National Center on Addiction and Substance Abuse released a disturbing report. The center is a nonprofit institute associated

with Columbia University. The center is headed by Mr. Joseph Califano, who was Secretary of Health, Education and Welfare under former President Jimmy Carter. The center's survey, "Malignant Neglect: Substance Abuse and America's Schools," is based on 10,000 random telephone interviews nationwide with parents, teachers and students, coupled with reviews of outside research on the effectiveness of drug abuse education programs. They found that sixty-one percent (61%) of U.S. high school-age teens and 40% of middle school-age kids say drugs are used, kept and sold in their schools. This group also wants tobacco smoking and excessive drinking, by adults or their children, to be considered substance abuse.

Drug dealers do not discriminate against anyone based on age, gender, race, economic status, prison record, sexual preference or nationality. They, drug dealers, can honestly display the "equal opportunity employer" seal because they will hire and sell to anyone. Most students like for someone to talk to them and spend time with them. When their parents, relatives and friends don't take time to give them attention, they look for some one or something to spend their time with. There is at least one person in or within walking distance of your community that works full time, even on Sundays and Holidays. He or she is your area drug dealer. The drug dealer is always willing to talk to you for as long as you like, because he or she is working his or her corner. He leaves his corner for short periods of time for food, bathroom breaks, to hide his cash and restock his products. They have little or no knowledge of the drugs they are selling. Very few can even spell the name of their product. Most of our drug dealers are middle and high school dropouts: so, I doubt if they can read and speak Latin, the language prescriptions are written in. They carry their drugs in their pocket or other unsanitary places on their body, and count them out to you with their dirty hands. Most dealers collect your money first and they only accept paper. Paper money has been passed through a number of hands and is full of all types of germs. Most don't know or care about the expiration date on the drugs, the side effects ,the other drugs you are taking or your medical condition. They only want your money. Ask your drug dealer, a cool person under thirty whom you trust, to answer the following questions:

1. I have diabetes. I took 50 units of insulin this morning at 8:00. How many hours should I wait until I smoke these marijuana joints you just sold me? How many can I smoke at one time?

2. I take pills for high blood pressure. When I smoke this crack, will I have a negative interaction?

3. I had a heart attack last year. Is it OK for me to shoot this heroin you sold me if I only use a little at a time?

4. I took too much Ridlin this morning. Will these pink pills you sold me bring me back to a decent stage of equilibrium / balance?

5. I am taking the blood thinner Comudin. If I snort a few short lines of Cocaine, will it be OK?

6. These diet pills are really making me depressed. Will these uppers you sold me make me feel better?

7. Is it OK to drive my car and operate machines after using these red pills that you sold me?

8. I don't have enough money to buy food and your drugs today; so the food will have to wait. Is it ok to take these drugs on an empty stomach?

The answer to these eight questions that you will possibly receive from your drug dealer is" Don't worry about your medical problems or how much to take or when." "Just get high and enjoy yourself; it's all good"

Parents and other older family members, if you use drugs, drink alcohol or smoke, the younger family members will know and will sometimes follow your self- destructive behavior. You can't hide anything from them.

THE NEGATIVE ATTITUDE PROBLEM:
In New Hanover County, we have a zoo called the Tote Em In zoo. For years, they had a fully grown elephant that stood out front with one piece of rope tied to his leg and the other end tied to a wooden pole.

The elephant had the strength to pull that pole down and walk away, but he did not think he could. I was told, when the elephant was very young and weak, that a metal pole was driven deep into the ground and then filled in with concrete A very thick metal chain was attached to the baby elephant's leg and the other end to the metal pole. Each time the baby elephant walked out far enough for the chain to pull tight, he would stop because he did not have the strength at that young age to pull the metal pole out of the ground. The idea was fixed in the elephant's head that he could not go any farther than that chain allowed him. As time passed on, the metal pole and chain were replaced with a wooden pole and a rope. The elephant had developed a negative attitude.

People with extreme negative attitudes are most likely to fail to reach their potential and probably will live a short miserable life. Most hate themselves and most people around them. Most have a few people if anyone they trust. They don't make goals in life because they think they can't reach them. Most don't live by or respect the laws of man or God. They live for the moment and take from people whom they think are weaker than they. If they have a job, they will do just enough to get by. Most will blame others for the problems they encounter in life. If they marry, they will soon separate. If they are rich, they will soon be under care in a professionally staffed clinic. The rich will be classified in such respectable words as, stressed out, depressed, mentally challenged, not motivated and a substance abuser. The poor will be simply classified as crazy, lazy and a junkie. The poor will be put in an understaffed state institution or end up homeless. We will most likely hear them say, "I can't do this and I don't care." They have been told a number of times by family members, friends and the school system,"you are dumb and will never amount to anything."

THE PROBLEM WITH USING THE NEGATIVE WORDS IN DESCRIBING MEMBERS OF OUR OWN RACE:

When I hear our Black film-makers, movie stars, TV stars, singers, rappers or any Back person saying nigger, it's like feeling a knife piercing my chest. To me, this is one of the most degrading words that a person can use to describe a member of his own race. The other word is the proper name for a female dog used to describe our Black ladies. I will not print it, but it starts with the letter B. The "N" word has become so used and accepted by so many Blacks that some non Black singers have begun using it in their songs. When Black people say "don't go to nigger doctor, lawyer, real estate broker, contractor, CPA, store owner, restaurant or others, they are calling these highly trained licensed professional people incompetent / unfit. If you repeat a phrase long enough, it will be implanted in your mind and you will start to believe it. This is what the phrase "perception becomes reality" means.

James J. Hankins

THE PROBLEM OF GIVING HERO STATUS TO PEOPLE WHO DO NOT DESERVE IT:

The fact that a person excels in sports, music, acting or business does not make them a complete person. Some believe a person is smart because he or she made a lot of money. The media (newspaper, TV, radio and magazines) give some people celebrity status and quote them so they can sell their product or production. One famous basketball player said, "I am not a role model." Those words made headlines and I was happy to hear him say that. He is as he said only a basketball player. Some people young and old think that if a person has money he or she also has knowledge and that you should listen to him or her.

THE PROBLEM OF SOME FAMILY MEMBERS NOT REACHING OUT TO HELP OTHER FAMILY MEMBERS:

A true story was told about a little boy who disliked going to the family reunion every year. His mother asked why, and the little boy said, "I don't know which family members we are supposed to be angry with this year."Some family members only see and talk to each other once a year during the reunion. The only other time that they come together is to bury a family member. They talk about each other there by planting seeds of resentment in the minds of the younger family members. Some families have no connections except in name.

Some family members are parasites / freeloaders. Since about 1960, my mother's family, the McLain's, have had a reunion every year. The Hankins and the Bellamy families also have

Reunions, but theirs are held every two years. All adult members are expected to bring enough food for their family and about six others. The host family will rent a place, mail out directions, reserve motel rooms, provide soft drinks and all other items needed for this family buffet. Each adult is supposed to pay a small set fee to cover that year's expenditures. If there is any money left over, the family treasurer will use it for next year or a family emergency if necessary. There are some adult family members who never pay their fee or bring food. These freeloaders only bring some large empty paper platters and a large roll of aluminum foil. They not only eat free but fill the empty platters with food, wrap it with their aluminum foil, then take it back to their room for dinner. They are teaching their children and grandchildren "how to get over on others." The lesson the children and grandchildren learn is simple. If you are low enough to cheat your family, then you should use everybody.

THE PROBLEM OF MIS-MANAGING MONEY:
Some family members place too much importance on material things. They have to have a popular car, a new house, the best clothes, the latest hair style and be seen shopping in the upscale stores. They live paycheck to paycheck putting on a show. They are, as we say, living large although they know they can't

afford to. The parents don't tell the children how much debt they are in so the children ask for the best also. There is no written plan to manage their money and no savings to dip into when an emergency requires money. Some have no retirement plan other than what their company provides. Others will have to depend on social security after their working days. Some are not even preparing for their funeral. The family sometimes has to take up a collection for burial costs. Some with children have not started putting some money away for college.

In some families, one person makes out the budget, pays all the bills, handles the investments and insurance. He or she does not for what ever reason share this information. When he or she dies, all this information and experience is lost. The surviving spouse not only lost a loved one but his or her money manager as well. They are not ready to deal with death and take a crash course in finance at the same time.

THE PROBLEM OF NOT HAVING SOMEONE OTHER THAN MAN TO BELIEVE IN:
Family members that don't go to some place of worship are setting themselves up for a big fall. If you can only depend on man in times of trouble and confusion, you will be disappointed. Family members, who are criminals, tell lies constantly and are substance abusers believe they will never be forgiven by anyone, so they see no choice but to continue in their life of misbehavior.

THE PROBLEM OF HAVING LITTLE OF NO FAMILY TIME:

At dinner time, the only time most families are all together, too many family members go to their favorite chair and eat dinner while watching television. This not only has a negative effect on our practicing interactive social skills but also on our physical health. Many health care professions have suggested we never eat our meals while watching television. This practice makes it almost impossible for family members to share the good or bad experiences they had that day. There are few if any family trips or vacations.

In the old days, the 50s and 60s, we had one black and white television and one or two stations. We watched television together. Most programs before 9:00 pm were suitable for the whole family, to watch. After 9:00 pm, the children's bedtime, the adult programs would come on. We did not have remote control; we had to get up and turn the channel control on and off. If you were watching something that you should not have been, you had to get up real fast and cut it off. Those old timers kept themselves in good shape. Today, 2003, some of us have more televisions than family members. Each family member will go to his space and watch his color television alone. We subscribe to cable and can watch over 200 channels, many specializing in whatever we want to see at any time, day or night. We need the remote control so we can quickly zip pass some of the channels we don't want our children or parents to see. Have you walked into a room and a family member changed the channel real fast? Do you think they were watching something you would approve of?

The telephone also takes away from family time. When I was a child, we had one phone that was located in the hall. In those days the poor had to share their phone line with another person in the area. It was called a party line. When you picked up the phone and someone else was using it, you had to wait until they finished talking or ask them to hang up if you had an emergency. Sometimes they would hang up and sometimes they would not. You could listen to each others conversation if you wanted to. We had one phone number in the phone book.

Today, (2003), we have a phone in every room, including the bathroom. When we leave home, we turn on the answering machine so we will not miss any calls. We take our pagers and cell phones with us everywhere. It is not uncommon to hear a preacher or group leader remind everyone to turn off their pagers or cell phones. We will not only see John Smith's phone number in the phone book but another phone number with the same address that is for John Smith's children. The cell and pager numbers are not listed in the residential phone book section but some will leave these numbers on their answering machine message. If this is not enough, some people have call waiting so you will never get a busy signal. How many important family discussions are being delayed or abandoned because some family member answered the phone and spent fifteen or more minutes talking to someone about less important matters?

The time some families spend surfing the Internet makes the problems caused by the television and telephone look small.

THE PROBLEM OF NOT PARTICIPATING IN VOTER EDUCATION, REGISTERING TO VOTE, VOTING AND WORKING TO MAKE LIFE BETTER FOR ALL THE MEMBERS OF OUR BLACK COMMUNITIES.

Since the majority of us Blacks did not keep up with the issues, and did not register or vote, many good candidates we needed to make positive changes were defeated. Some of our elected officials cause some people to respond with a smile, then laugh when their name is called. It is normal to smile, then laugh when you hear someone say Bill Cosby, Robin Williams or Chris Rock. These are comedians, so you expect them to say something ridiculous and funny. When some people smile and laugh at the names of President George W. Bush, Senator Jessie Helms, Governor Jessie Ventura or the officials in Florida that certified that presidential vote count, we can see why the Unites States has so many problems and so few intelligent solutions.

On the local level, Wilmington, NC, we also have an elected official whose name will bring a smile, then laugh to a large number of people. His name is Mr. Edward B. Higgins, Jr. Mr. Higgins, an attorney, is a teacher at Cape Fear Community College and is chairman of the all-White Board of Education in

New Hanover County. Chairman Higgins wrote an article of over 500 words in the opinion section of our local White newspaper, *The Wilmington Star News*, blasting an editorial that he felt called the school board, in his words, amateurish. Professor Higgins pointed out that five of the seven board members had or have educational experience. Attorney Higgins has been quoted many times saying, "We don't look at race when hiring employees in our school system; we just look for the best qualified to lead, teach and guide our students."

Mr. Todd Berliner, Assistant Professor of English at University of North Carolina-Wilmington, wrote a letter to the editor commenting on Chairman Higgins' article. English Professor Berliner said, "If one of my Freshman Composition students at UNC-W turned in an essay with that many grammatical errors, I would be suggesting remedial tutoring." He also said, "I assume that the chair of the Board of Education makes some key decisions about our children's educations. One who can't construct a coherent sentence (and who apparently does not know that he can't) would, I hope, frighten everyone. (The newspaper said Mr. Higgins requested them not to edit his article as they had in the past, so they published this one as written.)

I would like to say that I, like Mr. Todd Berliner, am also frighten by this. I don't know what subject Mr. Higgins, Board chairman, attorney and professor, is teaching at Cape Fear Community College, but I just hope it is not English Composition. Is he the best qualified person for the positions he holds?

Far too many of us do not have enough working knowledge of the following which will one day have a profound effect on our live and the lives of our loved ones: Wills - Estates - Power of Attorney - Guardianship - Life, Health and Long Term Care Insurance, Medicare, Medicaid and Social Security Benefits.

1 Timothy 5:8 (Paraphrased) says: But anyone who won't care for his own relatives when they need help, especially those living in his own family, has no right to say he is a Christian. Such a person is worse than the unbeliever.

THE SOLUTIONS:

Ecclesiastes 3: 1-13

There is an appointed time for everything, and time for every affair under the heavens. A time to be born, and a time to die; a time to plant, and a time to uproot the plant. A time to kill, and a time to heal; a time to tear down, and a time to build. A time to weep, and a time to laugh; a time to mourn, and a time to dance. A time to scatter stones, and a time to gather them; a time to embrace, and a time to be far from embraces. A time to seek, and a time to lose; a time to keep, and a time to cast away. A time to rend, and a time to sew; a time to be silent, and a time to speak. A time to love, and a time to hate; a time of war, and a time of peace. What advantage has the worker from his toil? I have considered the task which God has appointed for men to be busied about. He has made everything appropriate to its time, and has put the timeless into their hearts, without men's ever discovering, from beginning to end, the work which God has done. I recognized that there is nothing better than to be glad and to do well during life. For every man, moreover, to eat and drink and enjoy the fruit of his labor is a gift of God.

A story was told about a father, mother and their two teenage children. The mother was planning to cook a cake for dinner. The children were bored; so, they volunteered to cook the cake even though they had never cooked anything before. The mother gave them the recipe and told them to mix all the ingredients together. Place the batter in a large pan and bake at 350 degrees for one hour. These two teens asked their mother if they could cook two cakes so they could see which one tasted better. The mother said,"Yes all you have to do is double the recipe." They doubled the recipe and were now ready to put the two pans in the oven. They turned the oven up but soon discovered it would only go up to 550 degrees. In order to double everything, they needed the oven to go up to 700 degrees so they could cook the cakes for two hours. They told their mother the problem and she called the father and they had a good laugh.

SOLUTION1.

It is time for parents, children and other family members to start practicing good communications. The parents must be clear in telling the children what the rules and expectations are for their family. In my family, I tell my son that he is a Hankins and Hankins are always expected to be successful.

My father, *Edward Hankins, had to quit school after he finished the sixth grade to help his mother pay the bills. He later attended barber school and became a licensed barber. He was the proud owner of Hankins Barber Shop.

My mother, Faldenia Hankins, graduated from Fayetteville State Teachers College. She taught special education children for over 25 years. Her special children learned to read, follow directions, solve problems and take pride in themselves. They also learned to overcome the labels the school and society had placed on them.

We know from research that children will rise up or fall down to whatever level you demand of them. If you tell your son he is no good and acts like his no good father, he will probably end up that way. If you tell your son "I love you, I am always here for you and I am expecting great things from you" he will probably, out of love for you, work toward greatness.

I have always been overweight. One year my weight was really going up higher and higher. My nephew,

Donnell Simmons, who was a political science major at that time, said to me in a politically correct way, "Uncle Jimmy, if you continue eating high calorie foods, you may clog up your arteries and contribute to an early demise /death." My Aunt Penny, who was in her 90s at that time, would, as we say, tell it like it is. Aunt Penny said to me "Boy you are getting as fat as a killing hog." For your information, people did not kill a hog until it reached a certain weight, the more weight, the more meat to sell or feed your family.

SOLUTION 2.
It is time for all concerned family members to stop cussing. We can and must use positive words. In the 60s, there were only two cuss words allowed on TV; but today, just about all cuss words are used. It is called the new morality. I once heard a sermon on the so- called "new morality. The preacher said, "There is no such thing as new morality"; " The things people are saying and doing were a sin in the days that Jesus walked the earth and are still a sin today. " The rules of social acceptability have changed in 2003 but the Ten Commandments are still the same as the day they were written.

As a teacher, I did not allow students to cuss in my class. Some years it would take two to six weeks to bring some students in line. I would tell them to think before they speak or they would be reported. I did not expect them to just stop overnight, but they had to show progress. Some had a serious problem because their parents used profanity. The first three times they cursed, I gave them the option to stand up in front of the class and apologize or be sent to the office on a conduct referral. The fourth time they cursed, I would either call or write their parents. The fifth time, I would give them a lunch detention or some other punishment. After that, I would send a conduct referral to the office. One principal said "Stop writing students up for cursing because they all do it." I told him if he did not enforce the school and county policy, I would report him to the superintendent and the Board of Education. He did punish the students I sent to the office and after six weeks, there was no cussing in my class. The lesson here is, if you demand respect you will receive it. Parents, please buy a Thesaurus for yourself and your family.

SOLUTION 3.

It is time for family members to recognize their real heros; The lady that gained 30 or more pounds and experienced physical pain for nine or more months to give you life; the man who got up with you at 3:00 am to give you a bottle of warm milk. My mother, Faldenia, and father, *Edward, worked very hard and brought us up in a loving, caring and Christian home. With their regular jobs as teacher and barber and their other part- time jobs, they sent all six of us through college. This was at a time when a haircut was $1.00 and teachers were more underpaid than we are today. We were given very few things we wanted while growing up as teenagers but we received everything we needed.

Our parents made out a budget to control the small amount of money we had. We were economically poor but educationally and spiritually rich.

There are two types of money, old and new. Old money is money your parents, relatives or friends leave you when they die. New money is made by hard work, a savings plan and sound investments. People with old money did not work for it and some people with new money were in the right place at the right time. Please, never assume money can make one intelligent. If you have any doubt, just listen to a few radio or television interviews of some famous athletes and entertainers. Do you ever wonder why so many of them go bankrupt / broke, but their managers and lawyers don't? These people will, for a price, entertain you for a few hours. They will be there for you as long as you can buy tickets to their event. They might even speak to you while you are inside their entertainment center for that day. They love you because you pay to see them and will say or do anything to keep you coming back. They are living their (fifteen) 15 minutes of fame. Your true family members will love you and help you forever and there is no charge.

The real heroes, people I know personally, in my life are my mother, father, brothers, sisters, wife, son, relatives and extended family members. They are the people who had the patience and love to stand by me during good and bad times. Because they shared their time, talents and treasures with me and prayed for me, I have reached this successful point in my life. My mother has four beautiful and wonderful surviving sisters from a family of 12 children. They are all excellent cooks, good listeners and very inquisitive /ask a lot of questions. They are all life- time members of the Nornngton AME Zion Church located in Lillington, North Carolina. A few individual words about some of my family members.

Aunt Olina McLean, now retired, lives in Durhan, NC. She worked in a hospital testing lab in Chapel Hill, NC. She was part of a research team that worked with rats in an effort to find a cure for arthritis. She always was the first one to visit whenever a family member was sick. She would drive anywhere the sick family member lived and stay as long as needed. She would clean their house, cook home-made mouth-watering meals and not leave until she had nursed them back to good health. She was and still is, when her health permits, our family nurse. My cousin Connel, who lives in Durham, NC, said, "Aunt Olina is not the best driver I have ever seen but the Lord is always with her because she never hit another car and always made it back home without a scratch." Aunt Olina's question is always: "Are you taking care of your health problems?"

Aunt Ophelia McLean, now retired, lives on the home place in Lillington, NC. She worked as a secretary for 40 years with the N.C. Agriculture Extension Services located in Harnett County, Lillington, NC. Aunt Ophelia has been and is like a mother to me and others. I lived with her for one year, my late sister

Barbara lived with her for two years while teaching at North Harnett Elementary School, and my cousins Vivian lived with her for four years. She reared my cousins Connel and my late cousin James (Skinny) from birth through high school at Shaw Town. If that was not enough, after retirement she helped to send her grand nephew, Lamont, through four years of college at North Carolina Central University. Aunt Ophelia is still an active member of Nornngton AME Zion Church where over the years she had served as secretary, treasurer, choir president, Sunday school teacher, trustee and member of various other committees. She is also a member of the NAACP. Aunt Ophelia's question is always; "Are you still going to church?"

Aunt Casco McLean, now retired, lives in Durham, NC. She received a degree in Cosmetology from DeShazer Beauty College located in Durham, NC. She practiced her profession full- time for a number of years, then worked part time. Her love of working around and conversing with young people led her to a full- time job in the athletic cafeteria at Duke University. Aunt Cat, as we call her, also helped in the rearing of her grand nephew, Ricky. After retirement she helped send Ricky through four years of college at North Carolina A & T State University. Aunt Cat's question is always; When are you going to get married or when are you going to bring me some more grand nieces or nephews?

Aunt Wiltric McLean Clark, now retired, lives in Cameron, NC. She took a course after high school though the mail for a job with the Post Office. She passed the final exam, but this was during the days of legal segregation; so, she was advised to seek employment in California or Maryland. She married Thomas Clark, and they moved to Baltimore, MD where they both decided that she would work at home. If you could taste Aunt Wiltric's good cooking, you would see why Uncle Thomas and their children wanted her to at stay home. After Uncle Thomas retired and became very sick, they moved back to North Carolina. Uncle Thomas died two months after their last daughter, Larthea graduated from high school. Aunt Wiltric put Larthea through four years of college at Fayetteville Tech and North Carolina A & T State University.

Aunt Wiltric's four children Vivian, Thomas Jr., Donald and Lartha are now all very successful adults in their respective positions. Aunt Wiltrice's question is always: "How is your family?" then she will call out each member by name.

My late sister Barbara Hankins Simmons, a teacher in Newark, N.J. and graduate of Fayetteville State University, died while her daughter, Nicole, was in the eighth grade. My late sister, Caroline Hankins Oliphant, a retired driver license examiner and graduate of Durham Business College brought Nicole back to Wilmington, N.C., where she and my mother reared her as their own child. Barbara's husband, a devoted father, James Don Simmons, supported his daughter both emotionally and financially. He sent Nicole through four years at Spellman College. Nicole now lives in Atlanta, Ga.with her daughter Nia. Barbara's son, Donnell, a graduate of Tuskegee University, now lives in Newark, N. J. Donnell has three children, Brittany, Kumani & Zuri.

My brother Charles Hankins, a graduate of Fayetteville State University, took early retirement from his job to help take care of my late sister Caroline and my mother who was not well at that time. His wife of 40 years, Doris, has and is still working with him all the way. His daughter, Tonya lived with our Mother for over two years after Caroline's death and continues to give loving care to mother today. Their son, Reginald attended Florida A&M University and now lives in Raleigh, NC.

My late sister Alice Hankins Jackson, a teacher in Gulf Port, Mississippi and graduate of Fayetteville State University, died while her son, Wanza, was in the seventh grade. Her husband Lawrence was in the U.S. Air Force stationed in Mississippi. Wanza moved to Wilmington, N.C.,where my late sister Caroline and my mother reared him as their son. One year later, Wanza moved to Myrtle Beach Air Force Base to live with his father, Lawrence Jackson. Lawrence sent Wanza through four years at South Carolina State University. Wanza is now a teacher living in Wilmington, N.C.

My late sister Caroline Hankins Oliphant graduated as a proud member of the Williston Senior High School class of 1962. Caroline continued her education at Fayetteville State University for one year and subsequently graduated from Durham Business College. She worked in South Carolina and New Jersey a few years before returning to Wilmington, NC. Caroline became very ill and was hospitalized for several weeks. The doctor discovered she had lupus and estimated her life expectancy from that point in 1970 to be ten years. Caroline's faith would not allow her to just feel sorry for herself; so, she used whatever energy she had to help others. She helped rear (raise) her niece Nicole, her nephew Wanza and her grand niece Nia. She worked for Vocational Rehabilitation as a Vocational Technician and became the first African-American Driver's License Examiner in New Hanover County. Caroline was a devoted member of St. Mary

Catholic Church where she administered communion to the sick, co-founded the Gospel Choir and served as chairperson of the African-American Ministry and Evangelization Network. On the civic side, she was a lifelong active member of the NAACP executive board, worked with the Big Buddy program, the OIC, the Democratic Party, and the Black Women's Political Caucus. She received awards and recognition for her service to the community at large and the handicapped from the Mayor of Wilmington, NC, and the Governor of NC. When I think of Caroline, I think of the old joke. The doctor gave her six months to live. She did not pay him; so, he gave her another six months. Caroline lived 28 years longer than the life expectancy given her by her doctors. There is an old Negro Spiritual that reads: "This joy I have, the world didn't give it to me. The world didn't give it; so, the world can't take it away".

Reginald Armstrong is actually my first cousin. His mother, DeEsther, died when Reginald was born. Aunt DeEsther told her husband Earl that if anything happened to her, she wanted my mother, Faldenia Hankins, to rear her child. Reginald kept his last name, but he was reared as our little brother. With the help of his father Earl, my mother and father sent Reginald through four years at Fayetteville State University. Today Reginald works for a computer firm as a manager and is married to Vicky Armstrong. They have one son Eathan. Reginald has two other children, Brian, who graduated from North Carolina Central University and Shakera, who attends a community college. Reginald Armstrong has four brothers. The late *Larry Wayne, Michael, and the twins Jerry and Terry Armstrong.

My first cousin Theodore Smith, whom we call Bennie, is and always been like a brother to me. He was married to my late cousin *Marjorie Moore Smith. Most families have at least one person who, can fix anything and is always on time. Bennie is Mr. Dependable in our family. Bennie did not belong to a church and for a long time never attended a church. I decided to try to convert Bennie because I knew it would be a shame for a good person like him to end up in hell. It took a long time, but Bennie did join my church, St. Mary Catholic. Although he is older than I, I am his godfather. His conversion was so good that my wife and I chose him to be our son's godfather. Bennie has now earned his fourth degree in the Knights of Colombus. Bennie and his late wife Marjorie had four children: Pat, Gwen, Teddy and Marshall. They are all now successful adults living in Wilmington, NC.

I will be talking more about my wife Faye Bellamy Hankins and my son James Edward Oliver Hankins II in the remaining chapters of this book; so, I will not go into a great deal of specifics at this time. I will point out that my son was named after three great men (role models). His grandfathers, Edward Hankins and Oliver Bellamy and his father James Hankins.

My wife Faye Bellamy Hankins has two degrees, a Bachelor of Science (BS) and Master of Business Administration (MBA). Faye also took and passed the North Carolina Certified Public Accountant examination (CPA). She is the sole proprietor (owner) of her accounting firm, F.B. Hankins, CPA.

SOLUTION 4.
It is time for all family members to become actively involved in education. The old African proverb: "It takes a village to raise a child" is the key to finding solutions to many of our family problems; but more important is education. Mastering the basics at an

early age will prepare our children to understand that learning is not a burden but a joy. When we tell our children to turn off the television and radio and not to answer the phone for two hours during reading time, we must do the same. Learning does not take place just in public school and colleges. The days of a person being able to work on one job for thirty years are over. We must all be prepared to learn a new way of working, and we keep our minds sharp by continuing education.

I will share with you the things we do in our family that we have found to be successful. My wife taught our son to read at a very early age. We always have reading materials in our home. There is little or no cost involved because you can check out books from the public library. Most libraries will let you keep them for three weeks. If you have a VCR, you can also check out tapes. If the library does not have the books you are looking for, they can borrow them from another library. You can make that request.

We go to open house at the beginning of the school year, second semester or any time a new teacher is added. We take our son with us to meet and talk to his new teachers. We tell the new teachers our son is an honor student and we expect him to remain one. If our son is not doing his work or causing any problem in class, we expect and welcome a call. Since his education is our top priority, we can and will meet with his teachers at their convenience. We also tell them that each night we eat dinner together and he has to tell us what he did in each class that day and any homework assignments. My wife and I happen to be teachers, but most parents listening to what their child did in each class each day can tell if the teacher is teaching or just doing busy work. We require our son to keep a copy of all graded work and tests. We keep a copy of each progress report and report card. We look very carefully at his attendance, incomplete assignments and tardiness.

Our dinner time is our family time, so we do not answer the phone. We let the answering machine record it. Our other family members that live in our area are told to say pick up if there is an emergency. After our son tells us about his school day, we each spend a little time talking about our day. Then we have a family discussion on any topic we want to discuss.

Regardless of what you are told by school employees or any one else, it is never too late to learn new study habits. Your children may have to step back and spend a longer time than planned for reaching their goals, but they would not have reached them anyway if they were not putting in enough study time.

To get the most out of out education, these three groups must take on the following responsibilities:

STUDENTS:

1. Always carry a pencil or pen and a note book to class. You must be prepared to take notes.

2. Respect yourself, all adult school employees and fellow students.

3. Give your friends the attention they require before and after class but in class your undivided attention must be on your teachers.

4. Choose your goal and take courses that will help you prepare for that goal.

5. Cut off the TV, radio, computer, phone and Internet for two hours every Monday, Tuesday, Wednesday and Thursday that fall on a school night. Use this time for reading, studying and finding solutions to problems. Write down your solutions so you can review them later. This will help to improve your writing, and reasoning skills.

6. When some "fool" accused you of acting "White" when you speak proper English, study, show respect for others and make the honor roll, tell them White people have different personalities just like Blacks. Ask them which White person you are acting like?

The late President John Kennedy, an intellectual person who believed all people deserved equal rights?

George Bush, an intellectual light weight son of a rich father who, without money, would have a hard time holding down a good job?

Or Tonya Harding, a figure skater, who was accused of having a friend break the leg of her competition in order to win a spot in the Olympics?

You tell them you are acting "Black" like:

(A.) Rev. Dr. Martin Luther King Jr. He studied and earned a PHD degree, wrote several books, was a very articulate preacher, won the Nobel Peace Prize and led a civil rights movement that made significant changes in the United States and the world

(B) Malcom X., who dropped out of school after the eighth grade. He at one time was a street hustler who committed all types of crime. He spent time in prison. Although he was physically in prison, he freed his mind by going to the prison library and reading. He read, learned to spell and memorized the meaning of every word in the dictionary. He went on to   become a very articulate minister and leader. He helped free other Black brothers and sisters from their substance abuse and other destructive behavior.

(C) Mrs. Carolyn Q. Coleman the epitome/ example of a strong determined and articulate Black Lady who holds a Bachelor of Science Degree from Savannah State College in history and a Master of Science Degree in adult education and community college administration from North Carolina A & T State University. She served as North Carolina State NAACP Executive Director, and is now a member of the National NAACP Board. Mrs. Coleman served as Special Assistant for Community Affairs to North Carolina Governor James B. Hunt. Carolyn, as she is called by friends and admirers, also led the NAACP's efforts in North Carolina to eliminate the at-large system of electing city council members, county commissioners, school board members, and superior court judges resulting in more than eleven suits being filed. These victories resulted in the election of ten African- American superior court judges and more than forty local elected officials and two members of the United States Congress.

(D) Tell them about your parents, family members or friends that are successful because they studied and received a good education.

7. It is ok to complain and question, but you must use your time wisely. I tell my students to take sixty minutes. Spend five minutes talking about the problems then fifty five minutes finding the solutions. When they spend too much time complaining, I hold one hand up and say "Your five minutes are up."

PARENTS:

1. Take the time and have your school children help you to find all the answers to the parent test found in the problem section of this chapter. Keep it and update it when necessary.

2. Do not allow the school system alone to decide how much and what type of education your children will receive.

3. Know your children's goals and make sure they are taking the right courses to prepare for them.

4. Check your children's home work and discuss it with them during the two hour shut down. Call on a relative or friend if this is a problem for you. Read something that will help you reach the next level on your job or something that will prepare you for a better job.

5. Look for a progress report every three or four weeks and a report card every six or nine weeks.

6. Remember the student voted the best dressed, best looking, most athletic and funniest are often less successful than the ones that earned academic honors.

7. Do not allow the school system to place your child in a special underachievers class unless you have had a second opinion from a professional not employed by the school system. This may be expensive but your child's future can and will be affected by the outcome. Studies have shown that Black students are more quickly placed in special education than Whites. Take out a loan if you have to for the test. The money you spend now will be small compared to what you will spend later if your normal child is wrongly placed in a special class and receives a limited education.

8. Take the time to meet face to face with each one of your children's teachers. Go to open house and parent/teachers meetings. If for some real good reason, you can't go, then send a responsible adult family member or friend. Most teachers will care more about your child and spend more time teaching him if you show them you care. Teachers are also human; so, most will encourage and demand good work from the children of the parents they met at open house.

9. Tape educational programs so you and your children can watch or listen to them when you have time or take time. Two programs I consider educational as well at entertaining are, The *Tom Joyner Morning Show and Oprah.*

Tom Joyner and his crew are more than just Disc Jockeys. Mira J. is the serious one, Miss Dupree and J. Anthony Brown are comedians and raconteurs / storytellers. Tom Joyner, multi-talented, is the high priest of radio. They award a $1,000 Mother's and Father's Day Prize every week based on letters from appreciative children. They give a grant each month to a single mother attending a historic Black college. They take one or more news items each day and break it down to show the true picture. They send money to students at predominantly Black colleges who are short of cash and would not be able to finish that semester. Tom has a foundation that gives scholarships to Black students. They fight racial discrimination and encourage their listeners to call or write the companies that are practicing it. They interview newsmakers from around the globe. They sponsor "Take a friend to the Doctor" and play a little known Black history fact every day. They have their "sky show" at Black colleges and collect money for them. They also support the United Negro College Fund which is in the capable hands of former US Congressman, Mr. Bill Gray- CEO. They have Tavis Smiley, who also has a scholarship foundation and has authored several books, call in two times a week for his hard- hitting expert commentary. The lessons are many, including caring, sharing, uniting the family, voting and being aware of what is going on around you. Their unselfish sharing of time, talent and treasures has made and is making a difference in the lives of many of our people.

Oprah's serious shows bring in the type of informed people any good teacher would invite to his or her class if he or she could. Her guests share their knowledge freely instead of just trying to promote their programs and or sell their latest book. The problems some suffer because of the many types of discrimination are discussed with a search for truth and solutions, not good sounding political correctness. The audience seems to be truthful in their questions and feel comfortable asking them. There is little or no feeling that the questions are planted or that the show is arranged for shock effect and ratings. On the personal note, Oprah is very generous in sharing her time, talent and treasure.

> 9. You and your children should, at a minimum, subscribe to and read your local or area Black newspaper. There are almost always two sides to a story. People who receive all of their information from the White newspaper, radio and television are receiving one side of an issue because they are mostly controlled by large corporations. There are some products, families and people they are not allowed to question. The Black press, on the other hand, receives little or no money from large corporations, so it is free to tell the truth without fear or favor.

There are many Black columnists who put their job and or business on the line every day because they tell it like it is. They bring respect to a profession which is speedily losing it. I have a local, state and national must read weekly list. On my national reading list, these two men have appeared on one of the few television programs I watch: *Lead Story*, on BET. I suggest you watch and read Mr. George Curry, former editor of Emerge magazine and now a syndicated columnist and Mr. DeWayne Whickum, weekly columnist for *USA Today*.

OTHER FAMILY MEMBERS:

1. Box up your old magazines, *Jet, Ebony, Black Enterprise, Times and Readers Digest*, and mail them to a family member that has school- age children.

2. Have your old computer updated and give it to a family member with school- age children. This will allow them the same advantage their well- off classmates enjoy. Public school students are not required to do their work on computers but we all know that teachers will notice the   difference between a written paper and a computer generated paper. You can afford a new computer and you are just waiting for the old one to stop, so buy yourself the latest. This is a win/win situation.

3. Take the money that you would have spent on an expensive birthday or Christmas gift to an equally or a little less affluent family member and give the needed family member with school-

age children Internet services for one year. This can enhance their education and increase their pride.

4. Call them every six or nine weeks and ask them about their grades. When anyone from a student to a CEO has to give a report on his progress, most times he will work extra hard so he can give a positive report.

5. Help the parents find scholarships, grants and loans when their children, your family members, are ready to go to college.

SOLUTION 5.

It is time for the husband and wife to accept their different personalities and work to preserve their marriage. A story is told about a man going to a convenience store at 2:00 am. It had been snowing all night, the wind was blowing and the ice was starting to form on the streets. The man walked in and asked the clerk for a loaf of bread and a quart of milk. The elderly male clerk looked at the time and weather conditions, shook his head then said "Man, you must be married." The man smiled and said, "Of course I am married. Do you think my mother would send me out on a night like this?" These two men laughed for several minutes at the joke each had made about two different generations of ladies. Most of the older generation of ladies before 1960 prided themselves on being good cooks and housekeepers. Most of the younger generation of ladies after 1960, hate to cook, and will say with pride, "I don't know how to cook."In the case of men, it was the hated housekeeping responsibilities that have changed.

Chances are, our mate will not be like our father or mother. We must work together and weather the small storms that can quickly turn into a category five hurricane.

My wife, with my approval, took a leave of absence from teaching for one year to go to graduate school for an MBA degree. East Carolina University is in Greenville, NC which was about 150 miles from our home in Wilmington, NC. She had to move to Greenville, so it was a difficult year financially as well as emotionally. We had a significant shortage of money that year, which we knew would happen, but we never lost hope nor faith. I told my wife not to worry about money because I am a child of the king. "My heavenly Father has silver and gold." My wife would say in a joking way" I sure hope he will soon give you some of it."

We must accept our shortcomings and, out of love, work together. We men may have to adjust to canned biscuits, frozen fish sticks, powered mashed potatoes and those buy one get one free canned collards as opposed to home made biscuits, fried fish, real mashed potatoes and fresh collard greens. The ladies must adjust to home repairs and yard upkeep being less than professional. Many problems will have to be discussed and compromises will have to come from both sides in order to make this partnership work. In most cases today, both the husband and wife are working outside the home and must share the cooking and housekeeping duties. When children are added to the family, these duties will escalate until the children are old enough to help. Dr. Martin Luther King Jr. once said in one of his sermons, "You don't look to find happiness in marriage, you must create happiness."

SOLUTION 6.

It is time for family members to spend more quality time together. The home should be a place where all family members feel safe, comfortable and loved. No matter how we are treated during our workday, the fact that we are going home for a pleasant evening should bring a smile to our faces. One hour during dinner, with no interruptions, can give everyone a chance to talk about their day and share some news. Family outings and vacations are also important. A call to a close relative or any family member that is lonely or sick is a good way of sharing. Learn as much as you can about your family members. You should know their likes and things they dislike. You should always take time to talk or just sit with them when they need a shoulder to lean on.

On your cleanup day, all family members should have some area of responsibility and take up the slack if there are family members who are sick. Sometimes extra jobs will pop up and I tell my son that we all have a little more to do. He will sometimes say, "Why do I have to do this." I respond with the words to a song, which was a favorite of one of our long- time McLean family friends *Jack Ridgell: "Must Jesus bear the cross alone and all the world go free? No there is a cross for everyone and there is a cross for me."

SOLUTION 7.

It is time for family members to believe in someone other than man. It is a well known fact that families that worship and pray together, stay together longer. Please consider the following when trying to convert one of your family members:

I heard a story about two college students who shared a room together. One believed in God and the other did not. They had long discussions, but neither could convince the other to change his mind. The non-believer would always say to the believer, "Can you see him, can you hear him and can you put him in your hands?" The believer would say, "No." Then the non-believer would say "Then how do you know he is real?" The believer would say," Because "I can feel him." The non-believer said, "That is not a legitimate reason to believe in a God just because you say you can feel him." One day the believer came home and found the non-believer rolling on the floor crying. The believer asked his friend what was wrong and he replied, "I have a bad toothache." The believe said, "Can you see it, can you hear it and can you take it out and put it in your hands?" The non-believer said, "No." The believer said, "Then how do you know it is a toothache?" The non-believe said," Because "I can feel it."

In the September 3, 2001, issue of *Jet* magazine, there was an article about a study released by the American Sociological Association in Anaheim, CA. The study states the following:

It's the people at the church who make the difference, says Calvin College sociologist Mark Regnerus, one of the researchers of the study. Religious communities emphasize and reward socially acceptable behavior which encourages keeping up in school, he says. Participants in the study included 9,700 teenage students in grades 7 to 12 from all religious backgrounds.

There was a man named Saul, from a city named Tarsus, who was paid by the government of Jerusalem to persecute Christians. He hated the Christians so much and enjoyed his job so much that he arrested or killed all the Christians in his area. If that was not enough, he got permission from the leaders of Jerusalem to go outside of that area to find the Christians that had escaped. He heard the Christians had gone to a city named Damascus. Damascus was the main center for caravans/open wagon trading. People came from all different areas to exchange goods and conversation with others in Damascus. Saul feared the Christian movement would convert other people and could start to spread to Persia, Mesopotamia and even Rome. His plan was to stop it by bringing all the

Christians back to Jerusalem to stand trial. On his way to Damascus, Saul was struck by lighting, fell off his horse and became blind. He saw a vision of the Lord Jesus who said, "Saul Saul, why do you persecute me? "Saul asked, "Lord Jesus, what do you want me to do?" Jesus said, "Turn men from the darkness of evil to the light of goodness." Jesus then said, "Go into the city and you will be told what to do." Saul was told, in another vision he had of Jesus that a man named Ananias would help restore his sight. After his conversion to Christianity, Saul changed his name to Paul. Paul went to the house of Judas, where God sent Ananias, a Christian who lived in Damascus, to heal Paul of his blindness. From that time on, Paul became an itinerant/ traveling preacher spreading the good news of Jesus Christ. The transformation from Saul to Paul is a perfect example of what Jesus meant when he said to Nicodemus, "Amen, amen I say to thee, unless a man be born again of water and Spirit, he cannot enter into the Kingdom of God." He was often put in jail for preaching. With the help of Jesus, Paul performed many miracles and wrote many letters to fellow Christians. When he was placed on trial before King Agrippa II, Paul made such an outstanding testimony for why he was teaching Christianity that King Agrippa II said, "Paul you almost persuaded me to become a Christian." Paul, an ex-con, was found not guilty of any crime by Nero, the fifth emperor of Rome. In spite of this, Paul was beheaded some time later. You have heard or will hear the Apostle Paul's well-known words repeated at most funerals. I first heard these words when I attended my Grandmother

Sarah Hankin's funeral in the late 50's "I have fought the good fight, I have finished the race, I have kept the faith, now there is in store for me the crown of righteousness."

A large number of people that work in the field of Science don't have much belief in religion. They, scientists, want direct proof not circumstantial evidence. In the early days of the space program, scientists needed to have their time clock right before sending a rocket into outer space. Using their computers, they traced time back as far as they could go. They discovered that there was an interruption in time, but they could not find why nor when it occurred. An old Preacher, working as a janitor, overheard their conversation and suggested that they read from the Bible Joshua 10:10-14. The man of the cloth said "Pay particular attention to verses 13 and 14." They read as follows: (paraphrased / simplified) And the sun stood still, and the moon stayed, while the nation took vengeance on its foes. The sun halted in the middle of the sky; not for a whole day did it resume its swift course. Never before or since was there a day like this, when the Lord obeyed the voice of a man; for the Lord fought for Israel.

In my family, we use some old traditions like saying a Bible verse at Sunday dinner, praying before every meal, wherever we are, and saying a pray every night before going to bed. We also say what we are thankful for on Thanksgiving day and have the youngest reader read the Christmas story from the Bible on Christmas day. I added a new one. On birthdays, we have the youngest reader read the Psalm that matches the age of the person. For me, this year, 2003, my son read the 58th Psalm. The birthday person is encouraged to read and meditate on that Psalm a few times during that year. We believe a true Christian / Like Christ cannot just say a few prayers every day and go to church on Sunday but has to try to live as a Christian everyday. One Christian writer said, "Faith is the substance of things hoped for... the evidence of things unseen."

Mrs. Harriet Tubman was born into slavery in Bucktown, Maryland around 1821. Her early years as a slave were filled with abuse. It was at the tinder age of five (5), she was rented out to a White woman as a house servant. On her first day, before breakfast, Harriet was lashed with a leather strap four times across her face. At the age of seven, she ran away for the first time. As was the custom on all plantations, when she turned eleven, she started wearing a bright cotton bandana around her head indicating she was no longer a child. At age twelve, she became a field hand. She received a hard blow from a two-pound iron weight to her head by an overseer for refusing to assist in tying up a slave who had tried to escape. She would suffer periodic blackouts from that injury for the rest of her life. At age twenty five, Harriet married John Tubman, a free African American who did not share her dream of escaping north to freedom. He said he was fine where he was and there was no reason to move to the north. He also told Harriet that he would tell her master if she ran off. Harriet did not accept slavery or her husband's slave mentality so when she had a chance to run, she took off following the North Star that led her to Philadelphia, Pennsylvania. She was around thirty when she first experienced freedom.

For too many of us, that would have been the end of the story. The last sentence would have read, "and they lived happy ever after", but Harriet Tubman had another goal. Given her deep faith in God, she made 19 trips back into slave territories and freed her parents, relatives and others. These extremely dangerous rescue missions went on for ten years. This master spy/escape artist was so good at her work that at one point, the bounty for her capture was $40,000. The $40,000 in 1857 would be over one million dollars in today's money. Her passage way was known as the Underground Railroad which led over three hundred (300) slaves to freedom. She once pointed out to Frederick Douglass, in all of her journeys she "never lost a single passenger." In spite of the fact that she was handicapped with frequent long term blackouts and lacked the power to perform the type of miracles we find in the Bible, she was also called "Moses."

I believe our ancestors, the Negro slaves, had the same respect for our leader, a former slave, **"Mrs. Harriet Tubman"** as the Israelites slaves had for (the son of Yocheved) a former slave **"Moses."**

The words that Mrs. Harriet Tubman uttered in 1860 still ring true today. "I have freed many slaves and I could have freed more if they had realized that they were slaves."

SOLUTION 8.

It is time for family members to reach out to other family members. There is an old and very true saying:"Charity starts at home." My brother Charles Hankins graduated, cum larde/ with honors, 2nd in his Auto Machines class at Fayetteville State University in Fayetteville, N.C. He was placed with a large auto repair franchise in Washington, D.C. He worked there for six years then moved back to his home Wilmington, N.C. and worked for a large firm making boilers for thirteen years. His last job before retiring was for ten years with the largest electrical utility company in North Carolina. Each job was a move up in skill level and pay. Once a year on their birthday, Charles would give each of his nieces and nephews that lived in the Wilmington area a $100.00 savings bond to be used as a college fund. When Charles retired and had to learn to live on a fixed income, he could no longer afford to give out those $100.00 presents. I learned a great lesson from Charles, altruistic /charitable ways and with some changes I am keeping this family tradition going. Because of the ages and numbers, I am now buying bank stock for our grand nieces and nephews in my immediate family only. I do not give the stock to them but put it in their name under a dividend reinvestment plan. They will receive it after they graduate from high school and enroll in college. If they do not continue their education after high school, they must work on a job for one full year and receive a raise or promotion before they can receive the scholarship money.

When we have a little extra or some items that we plan to give away, we must first offer them to a family member. Some family members don't like taking what they consider hand-outs; so, be very careful how you approach them. The gifts you give should be between you and them only. Sometimes it may become necessary to delay buying something for yourself in order to give emergency help to your family members. Your children and grandchildren will most times treat their offsprings the same way you treated them. Please practice never talking negatively about our family members, unless they abuse people or drugs. If they have those problems, focus on them only and their need to get professional help.

SOLUTION 9.

It is time for families to learn and practice good money management. There are books that we can check out of the public library on how to make and stick to a budget. The members of the household should all know how much money is coming in and going out. We should learn about interest rates, investment plans, power of attorney, guardianship and insurance plans. Each member of the family could take one of these, do research, then share and discuss with the others. For books I suggest you read on money management, refer back to chapter one.

SOLUTION 10.
It is time for us to stop using un-prescribed legal drugs and illegal drugs. They both can cause serious mental as well as physical damage to our mind and body. Look in the average magazine and you will see beautiful healthy looking people, drinking beer, whisky and smoking cigarettes. On television, you will see the beer and whisky but not the cigarette ads. because they have been banned. In movies and television, you will see hoods and heroes smoking marijuana, using cocaine, crack, heroin and drinking beer and whisky. The heroes drink their beer or whisky in a mug or glass, while the hoods drink their beer from the bottle. The hoods don't drink those wimpy 12oz bottles, they drink the 32 oz (quart) bottles only. Research has shown that most of these ads for legal substances are made to appeal to young people and members of the Black race.

When I was in the Army, college and a few years after that, I drank whisky, beer and smoked cigarettes. I made a decision to quit smoking cigarettes in 1980 and stopped drinking in 1987 when I learned I had type 2 diabetes.

If we take a close look at the cost and medical consequences of our legal drugs, we would consider stopping.

If you drink a six pack of beer every day, it will cost you, on the average, $4.60 per/day. Most people eat something salty with their beer so, add one bag of potato chips per/day, which costs $2.00. The total for beer and chips per/day is $6.60. This is $46.20 per/week, $184.80 per/month or $2,217.60 per/year.

If you smoke one pack of cigarettes a day which cost $3.60 per/pack, this will add another $1,209.60 per/year. The total you will spend for beer, chips and cigarettes for one year is $3,427.20. This does not include the extras you buy on special days and holidays. I am sure you could find another place in your budget to spend or save that $3,427.20.

Payments for future medical problems will be higher for you also. The beer has about 145 calories per12oz can and the chips have about 960 calorie per bag. This is a total of around 1,975 extra calories per day from your destructive habit. If your normal calorie in-take is around 2,800 per day, you have only 825 calories to spread out for breakfast, lunch and dinner each day. This will call for a lot of salads with low calorie dressings and rice cakes. There will be very few calories left for grits, eggs, bacon, french fries, fried chicken, rice and gravy, or barbecued ribs.

According to reports from Surgeon General David Satchel, one of the high level Blacks appointed by former President Bill Clinton, legal drug abuse and too many calories can cause a number of problems, including:

ALCOHOL - and its affects on the following body parts:

A. Heart - Cardiomyopathy, a condition in which the heart muscles become weak and damaged.

B. Liver- Cirrhosis of the liver. A diseased liver can no longer process nutrients from digestion or break down drugs. Some symptoms include, fluid retention, swelling, jaundice and swollen abdomen.

C. Skin- it widens blood vessels at the surface of the body. Besides making you look flushed, this can allow excessive heat loss from body tissues, which may lead to chilling (hypothermia) and pneumonia in cold temperatures.

D. Brain- Alcohol has a depressant effect. Taken in higher doses it may cause serious problems with memory, concentration, judgment, coordination, and emotional reactions. Speech becomes slurred, vision is blurred, and balance is lost.

E. Stomach- A single heavy drinking session may give you the unpleasant symptoms of acute gastritis (inflammation of the stomach lining), which can lead to hemorrhagic (bleeding) gastritis.

F. In pregnant women, alcohol can increase the risk of damage to the fetus. The infant could be born physically deformed and / or mentally retarded. If a pregnant woman drinks even small amounts of alcohol, it can have adverse effects on the fetus and later, on the child's emotional and mental development.

OBESITY - The more alcohol some people drink, the more they pig out. Let us look at some of the medical problems we can experience.

A. Diabetes

B. High Blood Pressure

C. Strokes

D. Coronary Artery Disease

E. Kidney

F. Gallbladder

CIGARETTES - Smoking is the leading preventable cause of death in the US. If you are a regular smoker, you are probably losing about 5 2 minutes of life expectancy for each cigarette you smoke. Consider the average smoker, a person who smokes 15 to 20 cigarettes per day. Compared with nonsmokers he or she is about 14 times more likely to die from cancer of the lungs, throat, or mouth; 4 times more likely to die from cancer of the esophagus; twice as likely to die from cancer of the bladder; and twice as likely to die from a heart attack. Cigarettes are a principal cause of chronic bronchitis and emphysema, and having a chronic lung disease increases the risk of pneumonia and heart failure.

Some risks associated with smoking during pregnancy are:

A. Reduces fertility.

B. Interferes with the growth of the fetus.

C. Increases risk of complications.

D. Increases risk of miscarriage, premature delivery, and fetal death.

E. Increases risk of low birth weight.

F. Increases risk of respiratory distress

G. Threatens the health of newborns in their critical first days or weeks.

H. Increases the risk of sudden infant death syndrome

THE HAZARDS OF ILLEGAL DRUGS:
Any one of your family members who is dependent on illegal drugs endangers his or her health. In this lifestyle, overdoses are common and often fatal. Drug dealers often dilute a drug with a hazardous substance to increase profits. If the drugs are injected intravenously, the user risks bacterial or viral infection of the lungs, heart, brain, kidney, and other organs if he uses or shares contaminated needles and syringes. This puts the drug user at high risk of hepatitis and infection with HIV (human immunodeficiency virus, which causes AIDS). The drug dealers' ignorance, lack of self- respect and respect for others is only exceeded by the customers that buy and use their dangerous products.

You will often hear family members say: "I have a good reason for using this." I once saw a comedian on television playing the part of a drunk. The man with him was searching for a reason why he was so inebriated/drunk that night. The man asked him, "Did someone in your family die?" The drunk said, "No. "The man asked a second question, trying to help the drunk give a reason. He asked "Were you almost hurt in a serious accident?" The drunk said, "No." The man raised his voice and said "Why are you so drunk on a Tuesday night? The drunk said "I have a good reason for being drunk tonight, because, He paused, took a deep breath, then said, " I have been drinking all day."

We all know there is never a good reason to use self-destructive drugs. Drug addiction is not an individual problem, because all family members can and will be affected, directly or in directly, by it. It is a medical condition for which some insurance companies will pay most of the treatment cost. If you do not have insurance, call your local health department for directions. If whatever you have tried is not working, please don't blame yourself. You need help. The best thing you can do is seek professional help for your family member. Reaching for help is not a sign of weakness but a sign of intelligence.

Love, honor, respect, protect, pray for and support your family members. Establish good family traditions, because the younger members will follow your examples, good or bad. It is time to unite your family.

SOLUTION 11.
It is time for us to start functioning as first class citizens. We must make the important transformation from spectators in the seats to players on the court in all political decisions. We must attend all Board of Education, City Council and County Commission meetings. If we can't be there in person, we must watch it on public television. We who are church members, NAACP members, alumni association members and members of societies, fraternity or other organized groups must send a representative to all public meetings. We must educate first ourselves then

others on the issues affecting our community, then register and vote in every election. We must research and discuss the issues, take a position on them, then let our position be heard in public hearings. Every time they open the mike for the public to speak for or against, we must be there to express our position.

We must know who our elected officers are and make sure they know who we are. We must demand our fair share of jobs and services from the cities and counties we support with our tax money. The late President Richard M. Nixon even came up with a name for those of us who do not stand up, speak out or demand our rights. He took our silence to mean, that we agreed with him so he named us "The Silent Majority."

If you see a basketball player, rebound the ball, then start running a fast break to the other basket, and no player on the other team is trying to stop him, he is running to the wrong goal.

SOLUTION 12.
It is time for us to appreciate and work closer with our extended families. I have friends I have known from grade school and some from my college days at North Carolina A&T State University. I met Glen and Carol Mark in college. Glen was the best man at my wedding. We watch their two children, Tiki and Tre', grow and they watch our son Jimmy grow. We are a better people because we worked together so all could improve their position. Let us continue to love and respect each other.

Sirach 3.2-6, 12-14

"The Lord honors a father above his children, and he confirms a mother's right over her children, Those who honor their father atone for sins, and those who respect their mother are like those who lay up treasure. Those who honor their father will have joy in their own children, and when they pray they will be heard. Those who respect their father will have long life, and those who honor their mother obey the Lord, my child, help your parents in their old age, and do not grieve them as long as they live; even if their minds fail, be patient with them; because you have all your faculties do not despise them, for kindness to your mother and father will not be forgotten, and will be credited to you against your sins."

CHAPTER 2
WHAT OUR BLACK TEACHERS, COUNSELORS AND ADMINISTRATORS NEED TO DO.

"YOU SHALL NOT ACT dishonestly in rendering judgment. Show neither partiality to the weak nor deference to the mighty, but judge your fellow men justly. You shall not go about spreading slander among your kinsmen; nor shall you stand by idly when your neighbor's life is at stake. I am the Lord.

"You shall not bear hatred for your brother in your heart. Though you may have to reprove your fellow man, do not incur sin because of him. Take no revenge and cherish no grudge against your fellow countrymen. You shall love your neighbor as yourself. I am the Lord". Leviticus 19: 15-17

THE PROBLEMS:

Most Black Teachers, Counselors and Administrators in the New Hanover County School System are not in their position because they are wanted, but to help the system prevail in a racial discrimination law suit. When Black educators retire or move to other systems, they are almost always replaced with Whites. These well educated, highly skilled and often over qualified Black educators are treated as necessary evils. A large majority of Black educators fear any White that has authority over them and even some of their co-workers who are supposed to be their equal. This fear is evident when we hear them making these verbatim (word- for- word) statements:

1. I don't believe in rocking the boat.

2. You have to go along to get along.

3. There is nothing wrong with keeping the peace.

4. They want to run everything, so let them.

5. You can't fight central office.

6. If you make them mad, they will destroy you.

7. I don't feel comfortable questioning the people I work for.

8. I don't like the way they treat us, but I have no choice if I plan to keep my job.

9. Someone needs to do something to stop this racial discrimination.

10. I would tell them how prejudiced they are, but I would get angry, say too much and lose my job.

11. I don't like the way they treat us, so I am going to do and teach as little as I can.

12. They have always treated us this way, and nothing is going to change.

13. Those NAACP people are crazy; that is why they speak out and question school authorities.

14. I will never get promoted anyway; so, I am not going to waste my time taking extra courses.

15. I am too close to retirement to tell them off; so, I will just play this game by their rules.

The few Black educators that demand respect and file general and racial discrimination complaints are labeled and treated as troublemakers. A few are chosen as window dressers (appear to have power) and are appointed to subordinate (assistant) positions. The others are treated as willing second-class employees.

The following is a partial list of true examples of second- class treatment that I have seen and heard about from fellow Black educators in the last 27 years:

1. A Black teacher with twenty or more years of experience has to give up his or her class room to a new White teacher fresh out of college. The Black teacher in now floating from class to class.

2. Most department heads, regardless of experience are White.

3. There are few if any Black male teachers. If any, most are PE or elective teachers

4. Most of all head coaches in football, basketball, baseball are white, as are the athletic directors.

5. Most of the top level office workers are White.

6. Most of the cafeteria workers are Black, but most of the managers are White.

7. Most of the skilled positions in maintenance are held by Whites.

8. Most of the maids and janitors are Black.

9. Most of the teacher assistants are Black.

10. Most of the teacher assistants who are told about the process, encouraged to take part and given the opportunity to become teachers are White.

11. Most of the teachers who are sort out, encouraged and accommodated for the principal fellowship program are White.

12. The highest level courses, regardless of the teachers, experience, are taught by Whites.

13. Most of the in-school suspension programs are headed by Black teachers.

14. The Black teachers running the in-school suspension program receive little or no help from their fellow teachers, counselors nor administrators. Their assignment is to baby sit these mostly Black students; then recommend them for out – of- school suspensions. This helps justify the large number of Black suspensions because they are recommended and documented by Black teachers.

15. The Black vocational teacher is assigned another shop and subject in order to accommodate the new White teacher.

16. The Black vocational teacher is assigned the "problem students" that no other teacher is willing to teach.

17. If the new Black teacher is given a "below standard" evaluation in any area by the principal, most are not given a support team as are their White counterparts, and are not recommended for employment.

18. Most head counselors, regardless of experience, are White.

19. The Black counselors are assigned to the lower grades and are given duties that the White counselors do not want to do.

20. The Black assistant principal and counselor are rarely seen in a television interview, unless the subject is race or a government grant for minorities.

21. The Black assistant principal is in charge of free lunch, books, finding proctors for tests, bus duty, evaluating PE and electives teachers. He or she is last or close to last in the chain of command and seldom if ever allowed to serve on the budget committee or preside at an important faculty meeting. Most will retire as Career Assistant Principals. Some will move up to short term window dressing positions in the central office. They will remain in these positions until the White, whom the job is being held for, has completed enough workshops and is able to accept it. During this short term, the

qualifications for this job are being rewritten to match the person it is intended for.

22. The Black high school principal is an over-qualified PhD, is scheduled to relocate soon or is less than three years from retirement. He or she has a reputation of hiring very few Black teachers and is very hard on the Blacks he or she supervises.

23. The Black central office administrators are close to relocation or retirement, not allowed to make major decisions and are the lowest paid among their peers. They hire mostly Whites for their staff and attempt to justify their actions by saying to Black workers, "I have to be careful what I do or say or you know they will get rid of me."

The lack of respect and power given to Black educators is clear to all, especially the students.

When I was teaching at Roland Grise Middle School in Wilmington, NC a Black 6th grade student walked up to a Black assistant principal and said "I need to talk to the principal." The Black assistant principal said in a proud voice "I am one of the principals, what do you need?" The boy said "I don't want to talk to you, I need to talk to the REAL principal.

Given this type of treatment these educators receive and some accept, it is no surprise they pass it on to the Black students. If they do not have self respect, we cannot expect them to respect others whom they consider beneath them.

During my 27 years teaching in the New Hanover County School system, I have heard Black teachers, counselors and administrators make the following negative comments about Black students. These are verbatim (word- for- word) quotations.

1. I can't teach him if he does not want to learn.

2. Her mother is no good; so, she will be pregnant soon.

3. He looks like a drug dealer.

4. He lives in the projects; so, why waste time on him.

5. She has the morals of an alley cat.

6. Her whole family is a bunch of losers, and she is following in their footsteps.

7. His Father is in and out of jail all the time.

8. He can't read. She can't read.

9. Why don't they learn proper English.

10. They embarrass me when they open their mouth in my class.

11. They have an I -don't- care attitude.

12. They are so lazy. They slump in their chairs.

13. He needs to learn a trade, because he is not college material.

14. They don't do well in math.

15. Why did they put them in my science class?

16. He is sixteen; so, maybe he will drop out soon.

17. It is not my job to teach him to read.

18. I am going to pass him so I will not have to teach him next year.

19. She will never amount to anything.

20. I don't think he is worth worrying about, so just suspend him.

21. I can't afford to offend my White teachers.

22. Why can't they behave and study like my good White students.

23. They use such filthy language in my class.

24. She will end up on welfare.

25. They are not my problem

26. Some of those Black boys frighten me.

27. He looks like a gang member.

28. A good day for me is when he is skipping class.

29. His Mother has five children by five different men and did not marry any of them.

30. I think he is crazy.

31. If they can learn all the words to those filthy rap songs, why can't they excel in school?

32. These are children of unmarried teenage drop outs; no wonder they dress like trash and act so stupid.

33. I am not going to waste my time trying to change them. I have two years before I retire, so I will give them a passing grade and send these problems children on to the next teacher.

34. I am going to teach them the test, so I will get my bonus from the ABC program.

35. If the Church, their family and the school don't give them a good foundation, how can I teach them?

36. He looks and acts like one of those children from the government housing project.

These teachers, counselors and administrators have given up on members of their own race. This prejudging and condemning Black students after one or more unpleasant experiences is very dangerous. Most of us Black adults have expected and experienced negative treatment from most of the Whites in authority; but when we are treated this way by our own, the pain is deeper.

The responsibility that the Black Educators have or lack in their positions will determine the level of respect they receive from students, teachers, administrators and the public.

Some of our black retired teachers are 100% retired from education. They don't substitute, work in volunteer tutoring programs, or tutor relatives or their neighbors' children. Some travel and shop. A few spend their time watching "One Life To Live," Classic Sports and waiting to hear the famous words by McDonald Carey "Like sand through the hour glass, so are the days of our lives." Most will say, " I gave them thirty years; so the other teachers can help them now." This to me is tantamount (same as) to a retired minister stopping all religious activities. These teachers are letting 16 to 20 years of schooling and more years of sharing information, and further learning go untapped. Enjoy your retirement, you deserve it, but think about the type of life these children will live if they are not prepared. What will the days of their lives be like after going through an uncaring school system?

The final problem that I will point out is an obvious act of selfishness. As NAACP Membership chairman from 1985 to 2000, I mailed letters to every Black educator in New Hanover County every three years requesting them to join or give us a donation. Some joined or gave donations with the request that their name be keep secret. I did not appreciate their lack of courage, but I respected them for being honest with me. The educators whom I did not respect, are the ones

who paid their membership dues or gave donations until they were hired, transferred or promoted. After they were upgraded, they said in effect, "Forget about the other Blacks." Some were hired to teach; others were promoted to assistant principal, principal and positions in the central office. Some already in high positions, who had been paid far less than their peers, were given raises as a direct result of our filing complaints with the US Department of Education.

THE SOLUTION:

"The Lord is my light and my salvation; whom should I fear? The lord is my refuge; of whom should I be afraid? When the evildoers come at me to devour my flesh, my foes and my enemies themselves stumble and fall. Though an army encamp against me, my heart will not fear; Though war be waged upon me, even then will I trust. One thing I ask of the Lord; this I seek: To dwell in the house of the Lord all the days of my life, That I may gaze on the loveliness of the Lord and contemplate his temple, For he will hide me in his abode in the day of trouble; He will conceal me in the shelter of his tent, he will set me high upon a rock. Even now my head is held high above my enemies on every side. And I will offer in his tent sacrifices with shouts of gladness; I will sing and chant praise to the Lord. Hear, O Lord, the sound of my call; have pity on me, and answer me. Of you my heart speaks; you my glance seeks; your presence, O Lord I seek; Hide not your face from me; do not in anger repel your servant. You are my helper: cast me not off; forsake me not, O God my savior. Though my father and mother forsake me, yet will the Lord receive me. Show me, O Lord, your way, and lead me on a level path, because of my adversaries. Give me not to the wishes of my foes; for false witnesses have risen up against me, and such as breathe out violence. I believe that I shall see the bounty of the Lord in the land of the living. Wait for the Lord with courage; be stouthearted, and wait for the Lord."

PSALMS 27

First, a little background information on me and how I became a teacher. I graduated from Williston Senior High School, Wilmington, NC, in 1964. My friend, Chester Jenkins, and I signed up for the Army so we could attend college on the GI Bll after our three-year tour of duty. We took basic training together at Ft. Gordon in Georgia. After basic training, we specialized in different fields. I was sent to the infantry and Chester to electronics. I complained about my infantry assignment to the Company Commander but he did not change it. We both had signed up to go to Europe so they said the choice of work assignment was up to the Army. I did not like being in the infantry, but I gave it my best effort. During my second year, I was promoted to Sgt. (E-5) and became a squad leader. We completed our tour of duty in Europe then came back to Wilmington, NC.

We traveled to Greensboro, NC and enrolled in North Carolina A & T State University. I majored in Construction and Chester in Electronics. We both graduated with a BS degree in 1971. After graduation, Chester married his college sweetheart, Cassandra. I had planned to use my Construction degree to work for a construction company first as an assistant construction superintendent, then, after a few years, superintendent. This was the path to the top for Whites, but not for Blacks. I applied for many jobs but none would hire me as an assistant. After completing four years of college, I was qualified to work with my mind, rather than primarily with my hands as they expected me to do. I have nothing against anyone working with his hands; I admire and appreciate skilled workers. I love to do carpentry work, but I wanted the same opportunities in management that they gave to White graduates.

After working a few jobs in construction, I was offered a job teaching wood shop in my old school, Williston Senior High in Wilmington, NC. Mr. Leo Shepard, a civil right leader who also ran a job program, recommended me for the job and arranged my interview. Teaching was not a part of my plans, but I decided to give it a try. I found out that teaching is the second highest calling a person can have after religion. For the next 27 years, I worked to be the best teacher I could be. I taught in two middle schools and three high schools. In every school, I would put my favorite saying on the wall, "YES I CAN."I told my students they could do any thing that I assigned them to do. I did not allow them to use the word "can't" in my class. I would make them say, "I am having a problem but I can and will solve it." I told my students that three things were necessary for learning to take place in my classroom. A good Teacher, the proper tools and a student wanting to learn. The first two are always present in my classroom. Only they, the students, could complete the triangle.

While at A&T, I took a course in Real Estate and later; while working, I took and passed the North Carolina Real Estate Brokers' exam. Three years before retiring, I took and passed the North Carolina General Contractors' exam. I have worked for other Real Estate Companies since 1972 but in 1990 I started my own company, J. Hankins Realty, and one day soon I will open J. Hankins Construction. I will specialize in affordable homes for low income families. I will take Black students who dropped out of school, and are facing long term suspension or expulsion into my company's residential construction training program. I will give them something that we all need, a second and sometimes a third or fourth chance.

Two new terms or classifications were coined (created) during the civil rights movement- Freedom Riders (Fighters) and Free Riders.

Freedom Riders (Fighters) demonstrated by carrying signs in front of businesses that practiced racial discrimination and demanded that elected officers change unjust laws. We were sometimes beaten and put in jail. I was never beaten, but I am very proud to say I was arrested two times for demonstrating. We put our jobs and lives on the line to help bring about a better day for our fellow Black brothers and sisters.

Free Riders did nothing to challenge racial discrimination. In fact, most of them were what we call "Uncle Toms (people who bow, smile at White people and sell out their race). During times of slavery, they would be called house slaves. They waited until we forced the people in power to open up some job opportunities; then they applied for the jobs. They will tell you that they were hired because they were qualified. Indeed they were; but, so were Blacks fifty years ago. But no one was hired until we Freedom Fighters stood up and demanded our rights.

1. Before we attempt to work with teachers, students, parents and the general public, we must first practice self- purification.

   A. We must wash away all fear of white Board members, administrators, supervisors and peers.

   B. We must wash away all fear of white students, parents and the general public.

   C. We must wash away all fear of and prejudice toward Black administrators, students and parents.

   D. We must love ourselves.

   E. We must be better prepared than our White peers.

2. The story is told about a teacher who always taught the advanced math classes. This teacher questioned the principal's decision in a faculty meeting. Most principals resent being questioned by teachers; so they punish them by giving them a "slow class." The next school year, that teacher, as predicted, was assigned a

special class. These students were all identified as behavior problems and none had passed the end -of -year test. The teacher requested their records so she could prepare to teach them; but the principal refused and put all the special class records in a file cabinet in his office. One day while the principal was out of his office, the teacher took a quick look in her students' files. She had to work fast, so she just looked at their I Q (intelligence quotient) scores. The scores started at 100 and went as high as 118. The teacher went back to her class and said, "You are all intelligent students and I expect all of you to stop your lazy ways and live up to your potential." At mid-term, all her students were mastering around 75 percent of the same lessons she had taught her advanced students. By the end of the year, they had mastered 94 percent of the lesson and all passed the end of the year test. The school secretary told the teacher, "I saw you go in the principal's office and look in your students' files. What did you find and how did you manage to turn those D students into A students?" The teacher said "After seeing their high I Q scores, I knew they could learn; so I taught them as I did my advanced students. I refused to accept any excuses." The secretary laughed, shook her head and said, "Those were not their I Q scores. We did not put the I Q scores in their files. The numbers you saw were their locker numbers. The principal was trying to punish you, but it turned out to be a blessing in disguise for you and the students. The moral of this story is: "Students will do whatever we expect them to do."

Another valuable lesson we can take from this story is the fact that administrators should assign their best teachers to the students needing the most help.

3. We must spend maximum time on what we can change as a school. We have no power to change our students' neighborhoods, their family structures, the way they dress, their music or the movies they see. We can and must teach the following:

A. The importance of a positive attitude.

B. Our non-acceptance of profanity (cussing) in our schools.

C. Our non-acceptance of broken English. We must correct them. If we do not, who will?

D. The importance of taking good notes, developing good study habits and doing homework.

E. The importance of treating students, teachers and everybody with respect.

F. Go to school and to class on time.

G. Plan their work, then work their plan.

H. Choose classes that will help them reach their goals.

I. The dangers of illegal drugs and alcohol.

J. How to determine who is qualified to give them advice.

4. Make our lessons relevant (pertinent). Whatever lesson you are teaching, make a connection to something that is happening today. A farmer had a horse that would lock or unlock the door to his stall on a signal from the farmer. The farmer's friends asked, "How did you teach your horse that trick?" The farmer told his friends to watch. He took a 2 x 4 and hit the horse on his head. He then said, "First you have to get his attention, then you can teach him anything." Other than the 2 x 4, we must do what we must to get our students' attention. We want them to respect us and our programs; so we must respect some of their amusements away from school. We listened to Redd Foxx, Marvin Gaye, Tina Turner and James Brown. Can't we spend a little time listening to their Chris Rock, LL Cool J, Lil' Kim and Snoop Dogg? All rap is not filthy and negative but we will not know this unless we take time and listen to some.

5. Prepare ourselves for advancements. We must not hide our talents; nor should we allow anyone else to hide them. If we are the most qualified for head coach, department head, assistant principal, principal, supervisor, assistant superintendent or superintendent, we must apply for the position. If we are not given an interview, we should write a letter to the personnel director with a carbon copy to the superintendent asking why. If we are refused an interview more than once, we should spell it out in our letter. We must review our records at central office at least every two years to see if there is any thing in them to prevent us from advancing. We should walk into the central office personnel department with all our identifications and request to see our records. If we go in unannounced, they will not have time to add or take away anything from our folder. We must never accept a negative evaluation in any area unless we are guilty. We must write a rebuttal and request a conference with the person or persons who signed it.

6. We must stop accepting the small classroom, small office, oldest car, smallest support staff, lowest salary, worst duty assignments, oldest computers, worst schedule and lack of respect.

I have met with the last two superintendents and suggested the following:

A. There should not be any schools in this system with an all-white administration.

B. The racial population in all schools of teachers and students should reflect the racial population in that community.

C. No teacher, Black or White, should become an assistant principal after just four years of teaching. They have not gained enough experience for leadership. Most White assistant principals fail for this reason. These White assistant principals are evaluating Black teachers and students.

D. The Principal's Fellows program (train teachers to become assistant principals) must be around 40% Black to make up for the shortage due to past and present racial discrimination.

E. The program that sends teachers assistants to school to become teachers must be around 40% Black to make up for past and present racial discrimination.

F. The assistant principals should rotate their assignments every year. This would give each assistant experience in every aspect of school leadership. At the end of four or five years, all assistants will have the experience to become principals. This would cut down

on the number of Black assistants that retire
as "CAREER ASSISTANT PRINCIPALS"

7. We must stand up and fight racial discrimination. The New Hanover County School System
has a long history of racial discrimination. The
first law suit to my knowledge was filed on March
12, 1951, by Dr. D.C. Roane and Dr. Hubert A.
Eaton Sr., both prominent black leaders. The
law suit was filed because the New Hanover
County Board of Education was violating the
1896 United States Supreme Court ruling in the
Plessy V. Ferguson case. Plessy V. Ferguson ruled
that Negro (Black) and White schools could be
"separate but equal." Dr. Roane and Dr. Eaton
complained that the Board was following the
separate part but the equal part was not there.
The Board, knowing they would lose in court,
entered into an agreement to make the schools
equal. In 1954, NAACP Legal Defense Fund lead
attorney Thurgood Marshall,won the Brown V.
Topeka Kansas, Board of Education case in the
United States Supreme Court. This ruling made
separate but equal schools illegal and called for
all public schools to be integrated. The problem
with the ruling that caused this integration in
the New Hanover County School System to take
over seventeen (17) years was the phrase "With
all deliberate speed." "which is another way of
saying, take your time.").In 1964, Dr. Eaton filed
another law suit, Carolyn Eaton et al (and others)
V. New Hanover County Board of Education

because the school system was not following the 1954 Supreme Court decision. The lead attorney was Julius Chambers. Attorney Chambers worked for the NAACP Legal Defense Fund. Attorney Chambers later became President of North Carolina Central University in Durham, NC. Dr. Eaton won his suit. Because of the New Hanover County Board Of Education's history of past and present racial discrimination, the judge placed the school system under a court order that lasted over ten years. The court order said in effect, "We do not trust you to practice equality; so, we will be watching and reviewing your decisions for the next few years." All of the details of his school law suit and other legal actions in New Hanover County can be found in Dr. Hubert A. Eaton's well written and informative book, *Every Man Should Try*.

The New Hanover County NAACP filed three complaints with EEOC and the U S Department of Education. Legal Services and others filed complaints. I filed three complaints against three different New Hanover County principals with EEOC and U S Department of Education. I had a total of ten principals during my 27 years. Two, Mr. Kenneth White and Mr. Dennis Brandon, were good leaders and tried to treat all with fairness and respect. There was one outstanding Assistant Principal, Mrs. Elizabeth Holmes, who was the epitome (model) of an excellent educator. The other eight principals would have problems running a self service laundry. I filed complaints to the superintendent and the Board of Education against six of these principals. All six were eventually demoted, put in to other positions where they failed to perform or resigned to avoid demotion. I helped them receive what is known as poetic justice (got what they deserved). One principal asked for my resignation during my second year. Another said I was disturbing the family atmosphere of his school. All eight gave me negative evaluations. I questioned and spoke out when I saw problems. I refused to accept their incompetence and unfair treatment. I filed a written rebuttal to any negative evaluation and sent a copy to the superintendent. I also reported all attempts of retaliation against me from administrators to the superintendent, Board of Education and the federal agency which had jurisdiction over that area. I always taught my students to stand up for their rights; so, I was practicing what I was teaching. I must point out that I did not retire three years short of 30 years (full) retirement, because of any pressure the school system tried to place on me. The pressure is always on the guilty party to justify their actions. The school system employees were practicing racial discrimination and I was fighting it; so, they lost sleep. When you fight the good fight and don't have anything to cover up, you can sleep well every night.

My brother, Charles Hankins, who has retired from his job early to take care of my late sister, *Caroline Oliphant Hankins and my Mother, Mrs. Faldenia Hankins, became very sick and was placed in the hospital. It became my time to accept the responsibility and honor to serve as a care giver to my family.

All of these complaints brought positive changes, but if more educators and parents had stood up and fought for their rights, we would have made more progress.

The progress we did achieve was because of the courage and hard work of a few freedom fighters and our Black newspaper, *The Wilmington Journal*. These freedom fighters did not sneak around and whisper about racial discrimination; but they stood up and fought it. They openly and actively worked with the New Hanover County NAACP and other progressive people to bring about change.

The Wilmington Journal published the true stories as they unfolded and wrote editorials denouncing racial discrimination at every level. Because it exposed open and hidden racism, some racist individual or group bombed *The Wilmington Journal*.* Mr. Tom Jervay, owner and publisher, and his wife Mrs. Willie Jervay opened up the next day and kept printing. The Wilmington Journal did in the past and does today publish the news according to their motto: "Without fear or favor." *The Wilmington Journal* is now in the very capable hands of the oldest daughter, Mrs. Mary Alice Thatch. Mrs. Thatch adapted her father's award -winning editorial style. She listens to both sides, investigates, then prints the truth every Thursday.

In the race to end racial discrimination, you will find sprinters and long distance runners.

Sprinters jump in and out of the race as long as they are affected directly. Once they reach their selfish goal, they are out of the competition.

Long distance runners will run the race until it ends. Our goal also is to help our brothers and sisters reach the finish line.

The following is a list of some long distance runners I was privileged to serve with. I pay tribute to these cheerful givers for sharing their time, talents and treasures.

*Deceased

　　*Ms. Carolina Hankins Oliphant
　　*Mr. Reco Wallace
　　*Mr. Billy Burnett
　　*Mr Tom Jervay
　　*Dr. Hurbert A. Eaton Sr.
　　*Rev. W. Prince Vaughn
　　*Mrs. Doris Epps
　　*Mr. Harrie Reddrick
　　*Mr. Lee Shelton
　　*Mrs. Teresa Williams
　　*Mr. Tom Jervay Jr.
　　*Dr. Loroy Upperman
　　*Dr. Daniel Roame
　　*Mr. Burdell Harvey

*Father John Swift
*Mr. Andrew Bannerman
*Mrs. Dorothy Johnson
*Mrs. Rachel Freeman
*Mr. Joe Wright
*Mrs. Lorane Bethea
*Mr. Fred McRee
*Mrs. Barbara Hankins Simmons
*Mr. Edward Hankins
*Rev. James Steward
*Mrs. Alice Hankins Jackson
*Mrs. Marjorie Smith
*Attorney Lisbon Berry
*Attorney Robert Bond
*Mr. George Simpson
*Rev. Leroy James
*Mrs. Bessie Funderburg
*Mrs. Thelma Bull
*Mr. Horatio Forbes
*Mrs. Carrie Ballard
*Mrs. Eunice Boykin
*Mr.Hartford Boykin
*Mrs. Sadie Godwin
*Senator Luther Jordan
*Mr. James Brown
*Coach E.A. Spike Corbin
*Mrs. Cynthia Holmes
*Mrs. Faldenia McLean. Hankins (May7, 2004)
*Mr. Charles Hankins (April 6, 2006)

Mr. Glen Hughes

Mrs. Sandra Spaulding Hughes

Rev. C E Anderson

Rev. Lester Jacobs

Attorney William Fewell, Jr

Mr. Bernard Moses

Mr. Glover Melvin

Dr. Earl Sheridan

Mrs. Sylvia Colbert

Mrs. Ethel Lamb

Mrs. Marguerite Brown

Mrs. Willie Bradley Manley

Dr. Charles West

Mr. Lander Corbett

Ms. Evelyn D. Adger

Mr. Lewis McFadden

Mrs. Willie E. Jervay

Mrs. Doria S. Hankins

Mrs. Mary Alice J. Thatch

Mr. Cash Michaels

Mrs. Kitty Jervay

Ms. Shawn Jervay Thatch

Ms. Johanna Thatch

Mrs. Robin T. Allen

Mr. John McCoy

Mr. David Dowdy

Mr.Ricard Irving

Mrs. Geneva Clark

Mr. James Fasion Sr.

Mrs. Geneva DeVane

Mr. Reginald Armstrong

Rev. Jimmy Fasion

Mr. Tony Pate
Ms. Linda Pearce
Mrs. Burna Moore Horton
Mrs. Gracy Foxworth
Mrs. Sonja Green
Mr. Clayton Murphy
Mrs.Dorothy DeShields
Mrs. Bonnie Murray
Mr. Leo Shepard
Mr. Harry Forden
Mrs. Annie McMillian
Mrs. Faye Bellamy Hankins
Mr. Arnold Bryant
Mr. Lloyd Wilson
Rev. Dr. Lydia Atkins Wilson
Mrs. Johnnie Fields
Mr. James E.O. Hankins II
Mrs. Hattie Schmidt
Mrs. Lethia Hankins
Monsignor Thomas P. Hadden
Mr. E. B. Davis
Rev. L.O. Saunders
Mrs. Julia Bibbs
Ms. Tonya Hankins
Mrs. Mary Lennon
Minister Ali Kaazim
Dr. Diane Emerson
Mrs. Debra Gill Mason
Mrs. Inez Eason
Ms. Nia D. Satchell
Dr. Hubert A. Eaton Jr.
Dr. Suzette Stines

Mr. Harry Williams
Ms. Bernice Saunders
Mr. Anthony Josie
Mr. Joe Lamb
Mrs. Katherin Moore
Mr. William Billy Gibbs
Rev. Ann Garrett

Others not local:

1. Mrs. Caroline Q. Coleman - Former N.C. Conference NAACP Field Secretary and currently a member of the NAACP National Board

2. Mr. Enoch Parker - District Director, N.C. Conference NAACP

3. Mr. Eugene Gore - Past President of the Southport, NC Branch NAACP

4. Mr. Jessie Bryant - Past President of the Cedar Grove, NC Branch NAACP

5. *Mr. Earl Shinhouster - Past Acting National NAACP President

6. Rev. A.I.. Allison - Former Executive Director, North Carolina Conference NAACP

7. Mr. Nelson Rivers - National NAACP Director of Field Operations

8. * Dr. Lewis Dowdy - Former President of North Carolina A&T State University

9. Mr. Harvey Gantt - Former Mayor of Charlotte, NC

10. Mr. Julian Bond – President, National NAACP

11. Mr. Kweisi Mfume - CEO National NAACP

12. Mrs. Marliey Evers Williams- Past CEO - National NAACP

8. Demand respect. Two very intelligent and strong Black ladies served on the New Hanover County Board of Education at different times. They were ostracized (overlooked) and sometimes verbally abused by fellow Board members. In spite of the biased treatment that they received from Board members, school employees, parents, the public and the local White newspaper, they did not back down. These two ladies openly questioned the school system's discriminatory practice and made motions to correct them. They were not well liked by the majority but they were respected. After their deaths, two schools were named in

their honor- Dorothy B. Johnson Elementary and Rachael Freeman Elementary. We also have an elementary school named after the first person to file a racial discrimination law suit against the New Hanover County Board of Education, *Dr. Hubert A. Eaton Sr. With continued effort on our part, we will one day have a school named after *Mr. T.C. Jervay, past editor and publisher of The Wilmington Journal. Gallant (fearless) and caring people always rise to the top, despite attacks on them and their work. There are a large number of schools, scholarships, buildings and streets named after the late associated Supreme Court Justice, Thurgood Marshall. If he continues to vote as he is now doing, I doubt that anyone will ever name anything after Associate Supreme Court Justice Clarence Thomas or as his nieces and nephews call him, **Uncle Tom**. I read that one of his favorite Bible quotation is: Psalms 51:7 "Wash me and make me whiter than snow."

9. The Golden Package. The perception (impression) most people have of mail and baggage handlers is that they throw our packages and luggage around. A company once had a TV commercial about a golden package. This package belonged to the owner of the company and must be treated with care. Any employee found guilty of improper handling of this special package would have to answer to the owner. None of the company's employees knew when

they would handle the golden package, so they treated every package with care. As teachers, we deal with special children every day, because all children are a special gift to their parents. We may work for the Board of Education, but our ultimate (highest) responsibility is to the parents who trust us to teach and guide their children. We must treat all students, Black and White, with respect and leave the stereotypes where they belong, in the minds of fools. We know that prejudging is wrong, because most of us have experienced it in the past and are still experiencing it. We know from experience that students will do what you expect them to do. We as teachers have a responsibility to make our students better. We know some are- self motivated and others need to be pushed. Let us teach all our students as if they are our own children - "the golden package."

10. I attended elementary and high school during the days of legal segregation. The white schools were given the new books and equipment. When the books and equipment were worn out, they were sent to us at the black school. In 1954, while I was in elementary school, NAACP Attorney *Thurgood Marshall and others won a landmark case, Brown V. Board of Education at the U S Supreme Court. At that time, I was attending St. Thomas Catholic School (private) for grades one through eight. One year, we all had to go to the public school, because our church was building

us a new school. Our Priest at St, Thomas
Catholic Church was White but the entire
school staff from principal to janitor was Black.
We were taught by Nuns (a religious order). We
had great teachers at St. Thomas and found the
same good and caring black Teachers at Gregory
Elementary. We thought coming from a private
school with small classes, dedicated teachers
and strict discipline, we would be twice as smart
as those public school students. Today (2003)
that may be true, but in the days of segregation,
99% of all black teachers were good teachers.
Many black teachers lived in your neighborhood
and would walk by your house every day. They
knew your parents, relatives and your economic
status. They expected and demanded that you
do your best in school.

11. Hebrews 7:17 reads as follow: "You are a
Priest forever with the rank of Melchisedec."
Melchisedec was king of the city of Salem, and
also a priest of the Most High God. Melchisedec's
name means "Justice"; so he is the king of Justice,
and he is also the King of Peace, because of the
name of his city, Salem, which means "Peace."
High Priests could not become High Priests just
because they wanted to, but had to be called by
God. Teaching, in my opinion, is a profession
second only to the priesthood or the ministry.
Our Black retired teachers, if their health and
schedule allow them, must continue to teach
until they take their last breath. **You are a**

Teacher forever. Giving money to a scholarship fund or tutoring program is good; but sharing your knowledge and traveling experiences one-on-one is better. Studies have shown that some of the ailments we suffer from as we advance in age such as, arthritis, stress and depression can be lessened as we become more active. A few hours a week teaching or tutoring can be a blessing to you as well as the student. It is also reason for the retired men to shave at least twice a week and the retired ladies to wear one of the beautiful new outfits they bought while on a shopping expedition. Please don't forget that most of our Parents and relatives who worked long hours so that we could go to college (first family member to go to college for most of us), worked more than thirty years, and some were never financially able to retire. Please continue to use your gift.

It is ironic (unexpected) that my last three years of teaching were at New Hanover High School. This was the White high school that we at Williston (my school), received all the worn out books and equipment from. They had the best building, labs, furniture, buses and equipment, but we at Williston had the best teachers and caring parents. We did what was expected of us. The white principal of New Hanover High School in 1960 would not admit me as a student and the white principal in 2000 did not want me to teach in "her school." I know this, because it took ten days for my transfer from Hoggard High School to New Hanover High to be completed. The second day at New Hanover High School, I was called to meet with my Vocational Supervisor and the County Superintendent. The Superintendent and Vocational Supervisor told me that the principal at New Hanover High School wanted all the staff to work together as one happy family. They then asked me if I would work with the staff instead of speaking out. I told them the following:

1. I will do my best to teach my students, but I will not participate in any phony public relations activities.

2. I wear four (4) hats - NAACP President, Parent, Teacher and Tax payer. If I see something wrong or any one being treated unfairly, I would speak out. No one controls my freedom of speech.

3. There are only two people on this earth whom I consider greater than myself; they are God and my mother. All others are my equal and subject to questioning.

4. I follow these steps when dealing with complaints. I stop when I find justice. First, I talk to the person and try to either solve the problem or reach an agreement; second, I file a written complaint with the principal; third, I file a written complaint with the superintendent; Fourth, I file a written complaint with the Board of Education; Fifth, I file a written complaint to

the Government Agency with jurisdiction and demand an on- site investigation. Then I would file a law suit against the individual, principal, superintendent and Board of Education, if necessary.

I filed a complaint against her with the Superintendent my second year in "her school."

My late first cousin, Larry Wayne Armstrong, who worked in a very successful youth program, summed it all up in his favorite saying, "This is a hill for a climber; people with weak knees need not attempt it."

Black educators- if not us, who? If not now, when?

To read about educators who have been displayed in the national media for refusing to accept racial stereotypes, see:

1. Mr. Joe Clark at Eastside High School - the movie is "Lean On Me."

2. Mrs. Marva Collins at Westside Preparatory School in Chicago.

3. Mr. Vernon Jarrett - creator and national chairperson of the NAACP ACT-SO program.

4. For our Hispanic brothers and sisters- Mr. Jaime Escalante. - The movie is: "Stand and Deliver."

"THE LORD IS MY LIGHT AND MY SALVATION: WHOM SHOULD I FEAR?"

CHAPTER 3
WHAT OUR BLACK CHURCHES MUST DO.

"THE PROBLEMS WE FIND IN THE BLACK CHURCH TODAY"

"THE SPIRIT OF THE Lord God is upon me, because the Lord has anointed me; he has sent me to bring glad tidings to the lowly; to heal the brokenhearted, to proclaim liberty to the captives and release to the prisoners; to announce a year of favor from the Lord and a day of vindication by our God; to comfort all who mourn, to place on those who mourn in Zion a diadem instead of ashes, to give them oil of gladness in place of mourning, a glorious mantle instead of a listless spirit. They will be called oaks of justice, planted by the Lord to show his glory." Isaiah 61:1-3

When one is ordained to preach the Gospel, he or she is read this scripture to direct him or her as they walk in the shoes of the Fisherman. Rev. Martin Luther King Jr. used this same scripture in his sermon

"Guidelines For An Effective Church." Despite the road map laid out by Isaiah and Rev. King, most of our Black churches are failing to carry out its mission.

An article in the "CRISIS" magazine by Mr. C. Eric Lincoln, retired Professor of Religion and Culture at Duke University, and Mr. Lawrence H. Mamiya, Davis Professor of Religion and Africana Studies at Vassar College entitled "Does Crisis of Schism Challenge The Black Church?," made the following points:

1. At one time the black clergy were among the most highly educated members of the community, and a number of black colleges and universities were founded for the training of the clergy. This is no longer the case. The ministry of the Black Church is the only profession where only one of every four or five practitioners has graduated from professional school.

2. The membership of the seven historic Black denominations is composed largely of middle-income, working-class and middle-class members, with a scattering of support from poorer members, especially those in southern rural areas who tend to be among the most loyal members. But Black pastors and churches have had a difficult time in attempting to reach the hard-core urban poor, the Black underclass, which is continuing to grow.

Rev. Dr. Thomas Kilgore, former president of the Progressive National Baptist Convention, pastor and chaplain at the University of Southern California said ,"I see rough days ahead for the Black Church because of the following:

1. Selfish expectation of black preachers. What he called "the anniversary syndrome" - preachers wanting to receive money for whatever they do for people.

2. Failure of the Black Church to work for the renewal of the Black family.

3. Church leaders and pastors who are always seeking ways of raising money instead of just being good stewards.

4. Failure to understand the importance of supporting educational institutions.

Dr. Martin Luther King Jr. in his book, *Stride Toward Freedom,* stated: "Whenever the church, consciously or unconsciously, caters to one class, it loses the spiritual forces of the whosoever will, let him come doctrine, and is in danger of becoming little more than a social club with a thin veneer of religiosity."

Before I share my disapproval of the direction of the Black Church, I must say that I am not and never have been a member of a Black Church. I am a life long

Roman Catholic. My working knowledge of the Black Church has come from four sources.

1. I am the offspring of a religiously mixed marriage. Both of my parents are Black (African American) like me. My father, Edward Hankins, was a Roman Catholic and my mother, Faldenia Hankins, is an AME Zion Methodist. My mother agreed to let all five of her children be catholic but she also had us participate in programs and services in her church. Our parents gave us the best of both religions.

2. I spent my ninth year of school in Lillington, NC. I lived with my Aunt Ophelia McLean, also an AME Zion Methodist. I attended Sunday school, choir practice, revivals, testimonials and Sunday services at her church.

3. My wife, Faye Bellamy Hankins, and my mother had a few things in common. They both grew up on large farms, came from a large family, majored in education, became excellent teachers and are AME-Zion Methodists. I have driven my wife to many country churches on school nights where her choir and other choirs sang and the collection was divided between the preacher and the church. The traveling choir received a nice thank you and a request from God to grant them" traveling grace" on their late night trip back home.

4. In my capacity as an NAACP youth president, then as adult Membership Chairman, Executive Board Member, Vice-President and President during the last forty years, I often attended services and programs. We would always request money and participation from the Black churches.

My first concern is something I call the "Doctor (Dr.) Syndrome." In the education field, we finish high school, go to college for four years maintaining at least a C average, go one or two years for a Master's degree maintaining a B average, then two or three years of intensive research to write a theses (book for a PhD) maintaining an A average. Some of our ministers did not even finish high school, but call themselves Doctor. According to my dictionary, the Doctor of the church means a title conferred on an ecclesiastic for "great learning and saintliness." Taking a title that they did not earn is a bad example to set for members, especially school children. Scholars that earned the highest degree in their field are often quoted verbatim (word for word). I quoted four scholars early in this chapter. The writings and speeches of scholars are excellent references on their given subject. Some of their antithesis (opposites, unearned doctors), have problems speaking proper English; so I question how much "great learning" they've obtained. The Saints I read about sacrificed all material goods and helped to make the church prestigious. Some of the honorary doctors (unearned degrees) have become rich in material goods and gained their prestige by becoming a leader in an established church.

Dr. King once said that he spent a minimum of fifteen (15) hours preparing his sermons. If you really listen to a sermon by Dr. King, the text and the sermon will be forever planted in your subconscious. Most of these uneducated ministers never prepare a sermon; they just keep reciting well known verses of scripture and songs until the spirit hits a few members and then they push it to the limit. Rev. Martin Luther King Jr's. wife, Mrs. Coretta Scott King, called this type of preaching, whopping (talking loud but saying nothing). A member would say, "Lord that preacher sure preached today"; another member would say, "What did he preach about?" The member would say, "I don't know what he said but he sure did preach this morning."If your minister is guilty of whopping, it is your Christian duty to tell him or her. If it is not within your personality to tell him or her in person, then send an anonymous (unsigned) note. If no one takes the responsibility to tell that minister the truth, he or she will continue to preach in that style. Do you remember the text and the sermon delivered by your preacher last week?

Before delivering a sermon, some preachers will say a prayer. They will use one or more of the following familiar quotations asking God to:

1."Take me out of self"

2. "Lower me down into the storehouse of knowledge."

3. "Give me a double dose of the holy spirit."

4. "Grant me that power that makes preaching easy."

5. "Use me as your instrument."

6. "May the words of my mouth and the meditation, of my heart be acceptable to thy sight o Lord."

7. "Hide me behind the cross."

All of these are positive requests but then they turn around and start using excuses. To justify their failure to prepare a good sermon or their lack of confidence, they give one or more of the following excuses: "I have been in bed sick all week" "I have a bad cold" "This has been an extremely busy week" or "Yesterday was the first day this week I was able to eat solid food."

The members must stop excusing and making excuses for their pastor. If your pastor has a history of not calling, not visiting and not taking communion to the sick, you must question him or her.

The trial sermon is a practice that needs to be put under a very large microscope. The uneducated and untrained preachers that are ordained under this questionable process can be a liability (burden) rather than an asset (advantage) to their churches. After preaching for about six months or less, some of these preachers start their own church then, promote themselves to Bishop. Thirty years ago you would have to be a member of a big church or travel to conference once a year to see a Bishop who would be appointed by a board of Bishops to preside over ten or more states. Bishops make up a select group of very important people. Last week I saw three self- appointed Bishops in one day. In the bank, the fish market, and one at Food Lion. The new churches created by these trail sermon graduates usual have no dogma, (written rules or guidelines). If the preacher is a smoker, then smoking is OK Everything is based on the preacher's lifestyle and the way he or she interprets the Bible.

Shaw University, a very prestigious school located in Raleigh, NC, offers a Bachelor of Arts degree in Religion. Students must earn a grade of "C "or better in all departmental requirements, which include a shared core of ten courses as well as three elective courses and a senior project course in the area of concentration.

This is a sample of the type of required courses:

A. College English and Composition

B. Basic and General Mathematics

C. Introduction to Social Science, Physical Science and Biological Science.

D. Introduction to Computers, Religion and Philosophy

E. The Bible

F. Public Speaking, Humanities and World Religions

G. African American Religions

All of these courses and others must add up to 120 Semester Hours and four (4) years of college.

Have you ever known a person to fail their trial sermon?

Churches applying for and administering Government and private grants. Out of a $100,000 grant, how much is spent on the people needing help? In far too many cases, the preacher and his or her spouse pay themselves large amounts of money for positions they are not qualified for. Most of the other workers are not chosen because of their expertise, but because of their support for their preacher. Let us look at the following example:

A male preacher grew up sharing a two bedroom rented house with his two parents, brothers and sisters. The 1st bedroom was for the parents and the

2nd was the girls' room. Since there were no other bedrooms, the future preacher and his brothers had to sleep in the kitchen on rollaway cots. While living at home, he never took on a full- time job, but spent his time as an itinerant (traveling) preacher. When this man grew up, he became a pastor and moved into a parsonage. In addition to his generous salary, the church paid his rent, light bill, water bill, insurance, taxes and gas bill. His car, car insurance and gas are paid for by the church. He is often served food by his members so his food bill is very low. He has never had to rearrange his lifestyle or budget in order to pay bills or make a mortgage payment. Is he qualified to run a housing program that teaches people how to budget their time and money?

Studies have shown that the people needing the money from grants receive only about 30% or less. The other 70% is mostly wasted on white collar workers, long free lunches, travel, non-productive workshops, salaries paid for work not done and pay back to the professional grant writer. A small part of that 70% is paid to the people who perform some services to the people the grant was intended for.

Ministers and other high- profile members accepting positions on Boards and study commissions where they have no knowledge or expertise. They attend the meeting, look around and see that they are the only black on the board. Since they did not take time to research the issues that board is dealing with, they just vote with the majority. That Board has accomplished its mission. We once had a pastor who bragged about serving on nine (9) Boards in New Hanover County. He did not realize how he was being used.

Not including the children in all church activities. I attended a church service on youth Sunday and watched the children carry out their duties. They read the scripture, prayed, made announcements, took up collection and sang in the choir. The regular minister, an adult, preached a sermon. He thanked the children for being there and praised their singing but his sermon did not include them. I studied the faces of the children to see how many were paying attention to the sermon. During his hour long sermon, only two out of twenty children appeared to be in tune with a small part of his message. In education, we call this a teachable moment. The preacher had the children seated beside him facing the congregation. They did not have any paper to draw pictures or pass notes, any headsets to listen to music, or cell phones and they could not talk to each other. The preacher had a captive audience which could not leave, and failed to reach them with his sermon. When you have youth Sunday, preach to the children in some of their own words and phrases. Children are influenced by people and objects that they spend the majority of their time with. They spend hours talking to their friends on the phone, playing games, listening to music, watching TV and surfing the Internet. The church must find and implement programs attractive to youths.

For our Black senior citizens in Wilmington, we have Fannie Norwood Memorial Home For the Aged, Inc. My wife Faye gave all the residents a Christmas gift this year. This was the only outside gift some of them received although most attended church regularly before they became sick. I joined Faye in donating the materials to repair and paint all their front porch chairs. My woodworking class at New Hanover High School volunteered to do the repairs, refinishing and painting. We have over 100 Black churches in our county but not one has adopted the nursing home as an outreach project. The all- Black Greater Ministerial Alliance has made no attempts to service or support this final earthly home for some of their church members. I have heard many sermons about Jesus coming back to look for that church that is carrying out his mission. Our senior citizens are also looking for that church. Is there such a church in your community?

As NAACP membership chairman, I wrote a letter to every Black church. I asked them to choose one Sunday each year and take up a special collection for us. We also tried to get the churches to participate in our Mother-of- the Year Program and membership drives. About five churches, less than 5%, gave us limited financial support. Less than that participated in the NAACP membership drives. Many church members gave us money but told us not to expect a contribution from the church, because the pastor didn't like to see money from his members go to outside interest. That pastor has created an 11th commandment for his church: "All money raised in this church will stay in this church." Is this a New Hanover County problem or are other church members receiving this merciless (cold) message from their pastor?

The New Hanover County Youth NAACP was very active during the 60s. As one of the vice-presidents, I helped plan our "White Church Sunday." We put on our best Sunday clothes, divided into groups of eight and went to our assigned White church. After the Civil Rights Bill was passed, we were preparing to test all public accommodations in the county; so, we decided to start with our good white Christian brothers and sisters. To our surprise, we were accepted in every church without any negative treatment.

A little south of North Carolina, an NAACP group also tried to enter a White church. Three times, they were, spat upon, cursed at, threatened with bodily harm and turned away. They went across the street, knelt down and prayed. Their leader said, "God, three times we tried to go in that white church to worship you and three times we were turned away." Please tell us what to do. A dark cloud covered the entire block, then a bright light appeared as God descended from Heaven. God said, "Be still and listen to me. I have been trying to get inside that White church for the last 100 years, and they will not let me in either." Are there any Black churches in your community that are keeping God out?

This is a test. Please answer yes or no. Does your church have an ongoing program to:

1._____Visit the sick and take them to the doctor, grocery store, and transport them to church?

2._____Provide good clean clothes for the poor?

3._____Visit the county and city jails?

4._____Transport parents needing a ride to the school PTA meeting?

5._____Teach adults to read?

6._____Teach parents, relatives and others how to help children with homework?

7._____Give college scholarships to the members?

8._____Teach the young adults, boys and girls, how to care for a baby?

9._____Bring canned food every Sunday to be given to the poor?

10._____Give money to the NAACP or other civil rights organizations?

11._____Provide voter education? Tell members how to register?

12._____Encourage members to vote and transport them to the polls?

13._____Teach members the dangers of drugs?

14._____Teach and preach about all ten commandments?

15._____Teach teenage girls to say no to sex, and teach teenage boys to stop asking?

16._____Teach members how to budget their time and money?

17._____Teach members how to save and invest their money?

18._____Provide programs and services for the elderly and the lonely?

19._____Deposit the church money in a Black bank and use Black contractors and suppliers?

20._____Add new members and recapture the old members who have stopped attending?

21._____Encourage family participation?

22._____Include the children in all church activities?

"THE SOLUTIONS"

I offer the following suggestions on what our Black Church must do to save our people:

A story was told about a large group of people sailing peacefully across the water when a large log hit their boat. The log cut a hole in the boat and it started to take in water. All on board, except one man, were fearing the worst; so they started to dip the water out. When they were safely back on dry land, they asked the fearless man, why he was not afraid. He said:"The hole was on the right side of the boat and I was on the left side."

Philippians 1:27 reads: "Stand fast in one spirit, with one mind striving together for the faith of the gospel."

1. We need Faith, Hope and Love. My priest (Black/African American) Monsignor Thomas P. Hadden, pastor Emeritus (retired from active service)of St. Mary Catholic Church in Wilmington, NC suggested these three solutions.

A. "In order for a man to have a true purpose in life, he must first be a follower of Christ."

B. "If one believes in God and his teachings, our temporary life on this earth can and will be rewarding."

C. "You must love God, then yourself, then your neighbor. The triangle must be complete."

2. Deliver a good sermon. The church leader must be able to articulate (pronounce words and communicate the scripture using proper English) so that all members within the age of understanding will receive his message. If your leader lacks education and is under seventy (70) years old, then send him or her to school. A large number of Blacks over seventy were not given the opportunity to attend or finish high school. We have a pastor in the Wilmington community that was sent back to school by his members. That pastor is now communicating well and his church membership is growing each week.

The leaders must prepare and deliver a good sermon each Sunday. The other church leader have an obligation to tell that church leader if his message is being received. Failure to communicate is grounds for dismissal. Sunday school teachers must receive training in effective teaching methods. All new Sunday school teachers under seventy (70) years old should be required to speak proper English. This is not an attempt to fire good volunteers. Keep the teachers you now have and be thankful for them, but always strive for improvement.

3. The members of the church are responsible for the actions or lack of action by the preacher.

It is the members' responsibility to organize the church and plan the ministries it will carry out. The question each member will have to answer one day to God is not what did the majority do but what did I do? You may not be popular by your church standards when you reach outside the church walls to serve "the least of us," but you will be following a higher standard given to us in "The Beatitudes."

"Blessed are the poor in spirit, for theirs is the kingdom of heaven."

"Blessed are the meek, for they shall possess the earth."

"Blessed are they who mourn, for they shall be comforted."

"Blessed are they who hunger and thirst for justice, for they shall be satisfied."

"Blessed are the merciful, for they shall obtain mercy."

"Blessed are the clean of heart, for they shall see God."

"Blessed are the peacemakers, for they shall be called children of God."

"Blessed are they who suffer persecution for justice' sake; for theirs is the kingdom of heaven."

If the only people in the community that benefit from your "big church" are the workers that built it and stockholders in the local power company, your church is going in the wrong direction.

4. Let the worship service be 98% of the church hour and collecting money 2%. We say "Whosoever will let him come" and "Just as you are." I attended a church service once where every one had to walk up to the table and place their money. That collection took 30 minutes. Some people were embarrassed because they did not have what they felt was enough money to put in collection. Most people are more ashamed of being financially bankrupt (broke) than they are of being spiritually bankrupt. Don't let the lack of money or nice clothes prevent a person from taking a big step toward becoming a Christian. Let us make all people comfortable in church, especially the poor.

5. Three statements frequently made by some preachers are: "I don't care how many degrees you have, it ain't going to get you into heaven"; "I have the only degree I need a BA (Born Again Christian") and "I have Jesus and that's enough." The preacher is really saying three things.

I don't have a college degree: I don't plan to do the work necessary to earn a degree; so, I will insult the people with degrees. If you have Jesus, you don't need a degree. The preacher is sending out a negative message about education. If two people apply for a job that requires a degree, and one has a degree and one does not, but they both have Jesus. Which one will be hired? The mind controls the body. The mind is expanded by knowledge. Religion is not   physical but mental. An expanded mind will accept more religious teachings than a narrow mind. If your preacher does not have a positive educational message, dismiss him or her.

In order for me to maintain my reputation as a good teacher, civil rights leader and parent, I had to prepare by keeping up with current and past information. I found almost everything I needed in our public library during my frequent visits. I had either met or been aware of almost every Black minister in New Hanover County. I could count the number of Black ministers that I saw in the library on one hand. There was one Black minister I did see about nine out of every ten times I visited the library; his name is Ali Kaazam. I have the greatest admiration for Minister Ali Kaazam, because I believe he did his research and prepared a relevant message for his followers.

Teach each of the members the importance of basic and continuing education. Teach all adults how to help the younger members study. Develop a tutoring program for students and adults. Use your church bus or van to take parents or guardians to PTA meetings. Before the one hundred ladies in white or red finish their program, have each one choose one girl and be her Christian mentor (advisor) for one year. The men can choose a boy. This will give these children (And they are children!) something most of them are lacking an adult to talk to, to show their report card to, to answer to, and to pray with. These growing children will experience a Christian rite of passage and preparation for future responsibilities in the church and the world. Give every one of your college students a scholarship each year that he or she is in college. It can be as small as $25. The amount is not important. This will let them know that they are still a part of the church. Don't allow your college students to be among the group that says, "Good bye God, I am going to college." Give a Bible to all church members and each Sunday have one youth or an adult member who has just learned to read in your tutoring program come forward and read a few lines of their favorite passage.

6. One of the most important messages Rev. Jesse Jackson, founder of the Rainbow and Push Coalition, promoted while he was running for President of the Unites States was our need to register and vote. He said, "We are free to make our own moral decisions, but most of our economic and business decisions are mandated by laws."

Ever since my son has been old enough to walk, I've taken him to the voting booth with me. I've always told him the issues and the names of the candidates running for office. Our talks grew more interesting as Jimmy grew older and wiser. He started to form his own opinions based on his reading and observations. I let Jimmy mark my ballot and put it in the tabulation machine. My son does understand the importance of registering and voting. He had his registration form filled out and ready to turn in on his 18th birthday. We waited just before the polls closed to vote so we could see how the turnout was. It was low as usual. Indicating a Black church directly across the street from our polling place, I asked my son: "How many of those good Christians do you think took time to vote today." My son said, "I hope all, but probably very few."

The percentage of Black registered voters in Wilmington, NC, that voted in 2001 was less than 19%. The Black preachers, if they are interested, could change that percentage to 85% or higher. Any preacher who can convince a member, who is over $10,000 in debt and behind in their payments to contribute $50.00 or more extra money for the following fund-raisers: (100 ladies in red or white, Men's Day/ Ladies' Day, Pastor's anniversary, Pastor's birthday, Pastors appreciation, homecoming, tea, conference, and one or two special programs every month) could convince them to vote. Unlike the fund-raiser, there is no cost to register, and members can get a free ride to the polls.

They just need someone they respect to encourage them and tell them why they should vote.

Christ-like people must be involved so that when change happens in our political system, we can try to promote the change in a positive and equitable way. The constitution of the United States was written by imperfect men on paper over 200 years ago and, to date, has over 23 amendments / changes. The 10 commandments were written in stone by God over 2,000 years ago and there are no amendments. Teach your members to register and tell them why they should. Teach them how to select the right person to vote for. Teach them to vote in every election. Use your church bus or van to take them to the polls. Have a church or mass meeting at least two times a year with your elected officers for questions and answers.

7. Rev. Jesse Jackson, who also started the Wall Street Project, to bridge the economic gap between corporate America and minority communities, has said: "Black churches and members need to learn how to manage money." Mr. Jesse Brown, best-selling author of the book *Investing in the Dream: Wealth Building Strategies for African-Americans seeking Financial Freedom*, said "They take up a collection on Sunday, and all they do is put it in the bank and spend it right away. We want them to know they can invest and grow that money." The Rainbow / PUSH Coalition under the direction of Rev. Jesse Jackson and the New York Stock Exchange are

planning a conference to teach black ministers how to manage and invest their church's money. A second goal is for the ministers to pass on the financial education to church members.

8. Hospitals never close. Their mission is to provide physical care whenever and wherever needed. Our churches must be open to provide spiritual care when needed. Churches can pool their money and install a 24 hour call-in line. Programs for alcoholics and other serious addictions have phone lines for their clients to call anytime they need to talk. Is there any one on the line at your church?

9. Teach all members the importance of taking care of their Christian responsibilities. I attended a revival service at my wife's church, Christian Chapel AME Zion in Winnabow, North Carolina. The service was at night. I saw a man come into church with a very big flashlight. I wondered why he did not leave the big flashlight in his car. After church, I watched him walk out of the church parking lot, down a dark country road on his way home. He appeared to be under sixty years old so I imagined he worked his eight hour job, came home, ate his dinner, took a bath, put on his Sunday clothes and then walked a few miles to church. He was tired from working all day, had no car and had to get up early for work the next day. He had every excuse for not going to revival on a week night, but he came

anyway. It is dangerous to walk anywhere at night, especially on a dark country road. There is always a good excuse for not going to church, not preparing a sermon, skipping Bible studies, skipping revivals, skipping choir practice, Sunday school and not giving enough time and money to the church. Please remember this: Excuses are like aspirin; they give us temporary relief from our responsibilities. After the effects of the aspirin wear off, our responsibilities are still there. The person we are telling these excuses to may believe us but, like us, they will soon be dead. The final judge of our excuses died also, but he rose from the dead. He is alive, well and waiting for us.

10. It has been said that there are two types of atheist. Type (A) believes there is no God. Type (B) lives as if there is no God. We find a large number of type (B) in our churches who are Christian in name only.

On top of the steeple of some churches, you will see a cock (rooster). Jesus said to Peter " Before the cock crows twice, you will deny me three times." This cock is there to remind us of how many times we deny Jesus with some of our everyday actions. My mother-in- law, Mrs. Mary Holden Bellamy, is 89 years old. She has been an active member of Christian Chapel AME Zion for over seventy years. She believes that going to church and taking an active part in church activities is part of being a good Christian. Those who do not attend church and claim they are stay- at- home Christians will not have that support group most of us need to stay in line. If we are working to be Christ-like, our light will shine, and others will try to be like us. Lead, not by words but by example.

11. Unite the family. Have twelve (12) or more Sundays a year when one family would:

1. Read the Scripture

2. Usher

3. Read Announcements

4. Pray

5. Take up collection

6. Lead a song

7. Talk about the joy of being part of a Christian family

12. Preach and teach about the importance of following all of the Ten Commandments. A robber approached a man on a dark street, put his gun in his face and said,"Give me all of your money." The victim opened his coat so that he could reach for his wallet. The robber saw that his victim was wearing a collar around his neck. When he looked at the building behind

the victim he saw a catholic church. When the robber realized he was robbing a catholic priest, he said, 'Father please keep your money and please forgive me." The priest forgave the robber and offered him a cigarette to help calm his nerves. The robber said, Thank you Father, I would love to have a cigarette but I can't because I gave up cigarettes for Lent (Lent is a forty day period of sacrifice before Easter Sunday").

13. Expand the vacation Bible School from one partial week to many weeks of learning.

14. Use the grant money to hire a qualified manager to disburse it in the most effective way. Have the manager hire and train someone from your church to be his or her assistant. Hire and train other church members if possible. Give your members a written monthly report on how much money was paid to the manager, workers and all other people. This is a grant to a nonprofit organization; so all reports must be public. The only administrative people embarrassed about how much money they received are the ones who know they did not earn it. See who is receiving the most benefits from the grant money and make changes if necessary.

15. Ministers and others do not accept any Board appointment unless you are willing to research the issues and stand up for the rights of our people. Most organized Boards will send out an

agenda spelling out the issues a couple of weeks before the meeting. You can form an   advisory group from a cross section of the community to help you make the decisions. To remain effective to the black people you are representing, don't accept too many appointments. Recommend other black people that share your strong position. If they really respect you, they will accept your recommendation. Most Boards are aware of other Boards in the county, so ask yourself this question. Do they want my name and face or my ideals? Do not accept 30 pieces of silver for 15 minutes of fame?

16. Every church leader should read Rev. Martin Luther King Jr's. "Letter from the Birmingham Jail." This letter spells out the path Jesus laid out according to Isaiah 61, "The power of the Lord is upon me."

17. I have attended many quarterly (check-up) meetings in my wife's AME ZION Church. The Presiding Elder would ask the pastor the following questions:

  A. How many members died?

  B. How many did you baptize?

  C. How many joined the church?

  D. How many left the church?

E. How many special services did you have?

F. How many weddings did you perform?

G. Is your church prepared to pay your conference quarterly dues?

I would like to suggest that the Presiding Elder add the following questions for the pastor:

E. How many sick and shut-ins did you visit?

F. How many sick members did you take communion to?

G. How many food baskets and money donations did you give to needy members?

H. How many jail visits did you make?

I. How many, City Council, County or Board of Education meetings did you attend?

J. How much money did your church give to charity and outreach organizations?

18. "There was a certain rich man," Jesus said, "who was splendidly clothed and lived each day in mirth and luxury. One day Lazarus, a diseased beggar, was laid at his door. As he lay

there longing for scraps from the rich man's table, the dogs would come and lick his open sores. Finally the beggar died and was carried by the angels to be with Abraham in the place of the righteous dead. The rich man also died and was buried, and his soul went into hell. There, in torment, he saw Lazarus in the far distance with Abraham." Luke 16: 19-23

19. St. Francis of Assisi was born at Assisi in Umbria, in around 1182 and died there, October 3, 1226. His parents had both wealth and nobility. He could have lived the affluent lifestyle, but he had a higher calling. He made a decision to forego his inheritance, took a vow of poverty and founded the Franciscan Order. His Order not only taught the poor about God, but provided hands- on help to show the entire scope of his love. Francis is credited with many miracles and was canonized by Pope Gregory IX, July 16, 1228. St. Francis once told his followers "Never stop preaching the Gospel, even if you have to use words sometime."

Ministers and church leaders, practice what you preach. Every member, including the pastor, should make a written pledge to their church each year. This commitment to share your time, talent and treasure is not an option, but your Christian duty. To those whom much has been given, much is expected. Every one has either an abundance (lots) of time, talent or money, so share one or more with your church. The church should tithe (give 10% of its money). The 10%, or more, should go to members needing help, poor persons and outreach organizations.

The above list of suggestions can be done with very little or no church money. This can happen in a big church with a million dollar budget or a small church with a $12,000 per year budget. If your pastor is not working on a full- time job outside the church, he or she can do most of these on the salary you are now paying him or her. We make sacrifices for the people we love. We Christians must love our neighbors and follow the example of the Good Samaritan.

The Good Samaritan delayed his very important appointment and dismounted his horse on a very dangerous road to help a stranger. I once heard a Mission Priest make this statement about the Good Samaritan: "All the good acts the Good Samaritan did for the injured stranger happened after he got off his ass." (The donkey or small horse in those days was called an ass). He also said: "We Christians must get off our ass or, as others say, step out on faith and help our fellow man." Our main form of transportation today is not the ass (donkey) but the car. Our appeal to today's Good Samaritan (Christians) is as follows:

If you by pass certain corners and neighborhoods or speed up when passing by them, you will never be able to serve all of your neighbors. In order to take this important 1st step:

Bishop, Presiding Elder, Pastor, Preacher and Evangelist -Stop and get out off your Cadillac, Lexus, Mercedes, and Town Cars

Local Preacher, Apostle and Deacon - Stop, get out of your - BMW, Jaguar and Porsche

Chairman of the Board of Trustees, Pastor Steward, Sunday School Superintendent and Choir Director - Stop, get out of your Lincoln Continental, Chrysler and Volvo.

Ushers, Sunday School Teachers and choir members - Stop, get out of your Grand Marquis, **Van** and Sport Utilities

All Church clubs and members - Stop, get out of your Ford, Toyota, Honda, Chevrolet, Dodge, Volkswagen, Saturn, Pontiac, Nissan, Oldsmobile, Mazda and Buick.

There are no Black churches in Wilmington, NC, to my knowledge, practicing all 19 of my suggestions. You can read about some churches doing this and more in the book *IT'S ABOUT THE MONEY* by Rev. Jesse L. Jackson, Sr. and Jesse L. Jackson, Jr.

Other suggested books:

1. *STRIVE TOWARD FREEDOM* - by Dr. Martin Luther King, Jr.

2. *THE BIBLE*

My mother, Mrs. Faldenia McLean Hankins, and my father, Mr. Edward Henry Hankins, taught us to pay attention in church. They told us a good sermon has a powerful message. That message is implanted in your mind and will help you make good decisions when there is no one around to turn to. That relevant lesson will help guide us until we hear another one next Sunday and into infinity (forever). Over the past 50 years, I have tried to attend church every Sunday and on special days. I have heard many good and bad sermons. My definition of a bad sermon (no research, no preparation and no message) is one where the preacher reads a scripture, tells us his text (title), then preaches his sermon. I heard a visiting preacher in a local church tell us about how we should be like "Jabez." He says, "You know the story"which meant he was not going to give us any background information on"Jabez." I don't believe the average person would have know who "Jabez" is, to whom he is related, what period he lived in, his bad and good deeds nor what brought about the change in his life. The preacher then starts whooping until a few members get happy (loud answering, clapping, stomping their feet and shouting). He goes on reciting well known scripture and verses from songs. The spirit is in the church and the people have what the Apostle Paul called,"A zeal in Christ not according to knowledge." The congregation leaves a two- hour or longer church service filled with the Holy Spirit but no message to comfort them or to share with others. Jabez was still a stranger to most of us and probably to the four preachers in the pulpit who were jumping up and answering him as if he was really delivering a good sermon. I borrowed the Illustrated Bible Dictionary from my mother's house and looked up the name Jabez. It referred me to 1 Chronicles 4: 9-10.

As a teacher, I found six very important points that I would have used to transform Jabez from a name into a person. I will not explain each one, but I will outline them:

1. His Grandfather's name.

2. The name of his Tribe.

3. The type of delivery his mother had at his birth.

4. Why he was named Jabez and what Jabez means?

5. What he pray for?

6. What special grant God gave to him?

None of these were explained in the sermon. My question to my wife was, after being congratulated by four fellow ministers and probably all the other people present, except me, was: Who is going to tell him that he preached a poor sermon? Her answer was "Maybe no one."

The experienced church- going senior members (60 & older) must speak out and take the lead in bringing the Black Church back to its roots. The practice of good preparation must be passed on to the other members. The reason a 70- year old member will go to choir practice using his or her 50 -year old song book to practice a 100- year old song that they know every word of is because they want to do it right. When we demand that our pastors and other church leaders prepare and perform their jobs the right way, our Black Church will progress.

The following is a list of preachers I admire and respect. They not only leave you with a lasting message, but they practice what they preach by sharing their time, talents and treasures with the community. If Saint Peter had been sick on the day of Pentecost (3,000 souls were converted) and unable to preach, I believe he would have felt comfortable calling on any one of these twelve preachers / leaders to preach the Gospel that glorious day.

1. Monsignor Thomas Paul Hadden - Past Pastor of St. Mary Catholic Church- Wilmington, NC

2. Bishop T.D. Jakes - Nationally known Pastor, Author and television evangelist.

3. Rev. Lester Jacobs - Past Pastor of Price Cathedral AME ZION Church - Wilmington, NC

4. Rev. Joseph Lowery - Past President - SCLC

5. Rev. Ben Hooks - Past Executive Director - National NAACP

6. Rev. Jesse Jackson - Executive Director of PUSH

7. Rev Al Sharpton - Nationally known Civil Rights Leader

8. Mrs. Carolyn Q. Coleman - National NAACP Board Member

9. Rev, Dr. Lydia Aiken Wilson - Retired Master Teacher and now a full- time evangelist.

10. Minister Ali Kazaam - Wilmington, NC

11. Rev. Dr. Martin Luther King Jr.- Past President of SCLC, author, Preacher, Civil Rights Leader, and Nobel Peace Price Winner

12. Father John Swift - Past Pastor - St. Thomas Catholic Church - Wilmington, NC

And I point out to you a yet more excellent way. "If I should speak with the tongues of men and of angels, but do not have charity, I have become as sounding brass or a tinkling cymbal. And if I have prophecy and know all mysteries and all knowledge, and if I have all faith so as to remove mountains, yet do not have charity, I am nothing. And if I distribute all my goods to feed the poor, and if I deliver my body to be burned, yet do not have charity, it profits me nothing.

Charity is patient, is kind; charity does not envy, is not pretentious, is not puffed up, is not ambitious, is not self-seeking, is not provoked; thinks no evil, does not rejoice over wickedness, but rejoices with the truth; bears with all things, believes all things, hopes all things, endures all things.

Charity never fails, whereas prophecies will disappear, and tongues will cease, and knowledge will be destroyed. For we know in part and we prophesy in part; but when that which is perfect has come, that which is imperfect will be done away with. When I was a child, I spoke as a child, I felt as a child, I thought as a child. Now that I have become a man, I have put away the things of a child. We see now through a mirror in an obscure manner, but then face to face. Now I know in part, but then I shall know even as I have been known. So there abide faith, hope and charity, these three: but the greatest of these is charity....." 1 Corinthians, 13: 1-13

www.ingramcontent.com/pod-product-compliance
Lightning Source LLC
Chambersburg PA
CBHW061255280526
45784CB00002B/781